Praise for
Digging for Disclosure

"Our members, being both high net worth individuals and private investors, need to be wary of potential fraudulent landmines when investing. This book provides both a guide and resources of savvy due diligence practices to help navigate those pitfalls."

—**Jonathan L. Kempner**, President,
TIGER 21

"This is essential reading for anyone who wants to invest without losing their shirt the old-fashioned way—by getting ripped off!"

—**Jonathan Wald**, Graduate School of Journalism, Adjunct Professor, Columbia University, and former Senior Vice President, CNBC

"Worried about being defrauded? You should be! Former FBI Special Agent Kenneth Springer reveals the best tactics for discovering financial fraud—before you make the investment!"

—**Don Dixon**, Managing Director,
Trident Capital

"I believe in TIPS. Your tip to good due diligence is 1) T: Third Party Verification, which of course requires background checks of potential managers and business partners. 2) I: Internal Controls, making sure your manager's business has adequate internal checks and balances against member fraud, rouge traders, and so on. 3) P: Pedigree; who knows the manager or partner in depth and has done business with them in the past? And 4) S: Strategy; does the investment or business strategy make sense? Are the projected returns commensurate with the risks assumed, or are they too good to be true?

Surround yourself with the talent to assess TIPS factors and avoid making mistakes harmful to your career and financial well-being. Kenneth Springer and Joelle Scott will show you the way to succeed!"

—**Frank Casey**, Member of The Fox Hounds, SEC Madoff Whistle Blowing Team
Led by Harry Markopolos

"It would be nice to believe that federal and state regulators have the ability to catch investment frauds before the public is hurt. But, as we have seen time and again, regulators simply do not have the time and resources needed to catch all these frauds before significant damage is done. Investors must be responsible for their own money. This book is a vital resource for all investors to take control of their financial futures."

—**John D. Gill**, J.D., CFE, Vice President, Education,
Association of Certified Fraud Examiners

Digging for Disclosure

Digging for Disclosure

Tactics for Protecting Your Firm's Assets from Swindlers, Scammers, and Imposters

Kenneth S. Springer and Joelle Scott

Vice President, Publisher: Tim Moore
Associate Publisher and Director of Marketing: Amy Neidlinger
Executive Editor: Jeanne Glasser
Editorial Assistant: Pamela Boland
Development Editor: Russ Hall
Operations Manager: Gina Kanouse
Senior Marketing Manager: Julie Phifer
Publicity Manager: Laura Czaja
Assistant Marketing Manager: Megan Colvin
Cover Designer: Chuti Prasertsith
Managing Editor: Kristy Hart
Project Editors: Jovana San Nicolas-Shirley and Alexandra Maurer
Copy Editor: Language Logistics
Proofreader: Seth Kerney
Indexer: Rebecca Salerno
Compositors: Gloria Schurick and Jake McFarland
Manufacturing Buyer: Dan Uhrig

© 2011 by Pearson Education, Inc.
Publishing as FT Press
Upper Saddle River, New Jersey 07458

FT Press offers excellent discounts on this book when ordered in quantity for bulk purchases
or special sales. For more information, please contact U.S. Corporate and Government Sales,
1-800-382-3419, corpsales@pearsontechgroup.com. For sales outside the U.S., please contact
International Sales at international@pearson.com.

Printed in the United States of America

First Printing December 2010

ISBN-10: 0-13-138556-9
ISBN-13: 978-0-13-138556-6

Pearson Education LTD.
Pearson Education Australia PTY, Limited.
Pearson Education Singapore, Pte. Ltd.
Pearson Education Asia, Ltd.
Pearson Education Canada, Ltd.
Pearson Educación de Mexico, S.A. de C.V.
Pearson Education—Japan
Pearson Education Malaysia, Pte. Ltd.

Library of Congress Cataloging-in-Publication Data

Springer, Kenneth S., 1953-

Digging for disclosure : tactics for protecting your firm's assets from swindlers, scammers,
and imposters / Kenneth S. Springer, Joelle Scott.

p. cm.

ISBN-13: 978-0-13-138556-6 (hardback : alk. paper)

ISBN-10: 0-13-138556-9

1. Investment advisors—Selection and appointment. 2. Personnel management. 3. Disclosure of information. I. Scott, Joelle, 1974- II. Title.

HG4621.S75 2011

658.4'7—dc22

2010026248

Contents

Acknowledgments

We would like to thank the following people for their help and support over the years and for putting up with us during this process: the brilliant team at Corporate Resolutions, Inc., specifically Shelley Marinaro, Kayla Boorady, Richard MacDonnell, Kristin Wenske, Dan Vassallo, Laura Klein, Lauren Gumiela, and Don Klaskin; our amazing clients who have continued to put their trust in us; our dear family members and friends, including Mary Springer, Kenny, Jenn, and August Springer, Michael, Stephanie and Eleanor Springer, Billy Springer, Tom Springer, Martin, Miles and West McGowan, Richard Wald, Meghan Mayhew, Alexis Mintz, Jacqueline Klinger, Samantha Beinstein, Madeleine Perez, Howard and Karen Scott, Joy Scott, and, of course, our editors and publishers who were enormously patient and incredibly helpful.

About the Authors

Kenneth S. Springer, a Certified Fraud Examiner, is president and founder of Corporate Resolutions, Inc. A former special agent of the Federal Bureau of Investigation, Mr. Springer has conducted business-related investigations and intelligence gathering for more than thirty years. While in the FBI, Mr. Springer worked on numerous internal and external bank frauds, wire frauds, Wall Street-related crimes, and other complex white-collar investigations. Prior to founding Corporate Resolutions in 1991, he was president of Bishops Services, Inc., an investigative firm in New York City.

A 1975 graduate of Siena College with a B.S. in finance, Mr. Springer is an active member of the Society of Former Special Agents of the Federal Bureau of Investigation, the Association of Certified Fraud Examiners (ACFE), the Securities Industry and Financial Markets Association-Legal and Compliance Division (SIFMACL), the Association for Corporate Growth (ACG), the Association for Independent Private Sector Inspectors General (IPSIG), the American Society for Industrial Security (ASIS), the Managed Funds Association (MFA), Commercial Finance Association (CFA), and the European Venture Capital Association (EVCA). Corporate Resolutions is also a sponsor of the New York Private Equity Network (NYPEN), the HedgeFund CFO Association, and a recommended service provider of the National Venture Capital Association (NVCA). Mr. Springer is also a frequent speaker and lecturer on private equity, hedge funds, global due diligence issues, risk management, and corporate investigations.

Joelle Scott is the Director of Business Intelligence at Corporate Resolutions, Inc. Ms. Scott has spent the last twelve years in business investigations and currently oversees the intelligence analysts at Corporate Resolutions to ensure quality control and accuracy of all investigative reports. A graduate of Colgate University, Ms. Scott received her master's degree in journalism from the Columbia University Graduate School of Journalism. Ms. Scott is also a teaching assistant for Richard Wald at Columbia's Journalism School on the topics of Critical Issues in Journalism and National Affairs Reporting.

Introduction

"I should have done more."
"I did not even think to look into it."
"I didn't think this would happen to me."

No, I am not a psychologist, and these are not quotes from my patients. These are some of the painful comments made by investors who have been fleeced. Whether you have been monetarily slammed by Bernie Madoff or simply misled by a borrower, hedge fund manager, or executive with whom you have invested, the economic pain and embarrassment has the same pinch. As a former Special Agent with the Federal Bureau of Investigation (FBI) and the president of a business investigations firm, I have accumulated a number of preventive business methods that help investors of all sizes protect their interests and avoid being the victims of fraud. Even if you have made successful investments over the years and have, thankfully, not been ensnared in a ring of investment fraud, on any scale these methods illuminate the need for gathering intelligence to ensure you keep your track record. From my vault of cases I have investigated over the past 20 years, I have compiled these practices, lessons, and stories to share with you and hope you will arm yourself with these tools before making your next investment.

Financial and legal due diligence are accepted norms in the investment community. What is often overlooked, however, is the importance of conducting proper background checks on a management team, fund manager, or investment adviser. Background checks are your "people due diligence." The success of your investment relies *solely* on the abilities of the people (or person) who oversee your money. Although not a line item on the balance sheet of a company, management is your biggest asset. Unfortunately, many investors only realize this when damage has been done and liabilities are being tallied.

At Corporate Resolutions, Inc., the business investigations firm I formed in 1991, I have conducted background checks on thousands of individuals and companies. Three of the biggest mistakes that we have seen investors make repeatedly are

1. ***Flock Funding.*** Investors hire based on reputation instead of research (the perfect example is Bernie Madoff's affinity fraud). Everyone assumes someone else did the homework. If someone says, "He is well-known," "I checked them out," or "I know him; he is a good guy," what does that mean? The onus is on you. You need to do your own investigating because not everyone adheres to the same definition of risk (or comfort). Very few investors get cheated by people they do not like; Bernie Madoff's investors liked him. While Madoff did not cause a recession, he did cause us to reassess our processes.

2. ***The Bottom-Line Blockade.*** Investors tend to have blinders on. They are focused solely on the predicted returns of a deal and thus overlook the yellow or red flags that exist. Keep your mind open to all the information you can gather and remember that high rates of return on your investment are worthless if your money is in the wrong hands.

3. ***Precipitate, Not Investigate.*** Investors often move too quickly and do not take the time to look into an individual's background. We are all accustomed to making swift decisions and having information instantaneously. But when making an investment, you need to take precautions. A person's past performance is often indicative of future behavior. Although much information is available at our fingertips, it takes time to conduct an appropriately rigorous background check. References

must be contacted, degrees must be confirmed, lawsuits must be reviewed, media and Internet attention must be considered, and so on. These steps cannot be done overnight. As President Ronald Reagan used to say, "Trust, but verify."

Background checks are often viewed as deal-killers. In actuality, background checks rescue investors from inevitably explosive deals or even resuscitate investments that otherwise looked murky. As more state and federal regulations clamp down on the investment industry, businesses will be (and some already are) required to implement meticulous due diligence techniques. These techniques should involve a lot more than a quick Google search or simple check-the-box criminal record review. If you look at Bernie Madoff, Robert Allen Stanford, and Danny Pang, the perpetrators of three of the biggest investment scandals in 2009, you will find all three had something in common: no criminal record history (until now). This alone is proof that you cannot rely on meager background checks. Securing your investment is crucial; comprehensive background checks are your most reliable tools.

We have found that although a tremendous amount of information is available online, it is imperative to know what is *not* available. The gap between the two is wide, and the awareness of this will better serve you in your role as a prudent investor. As we detail throughout this book, the ability to identify discrepancies, vagaries, and half-truths is as indispensable as finding overt criminal record histories or regulatory problems.

That is not to say that glaring criminal records are not hazardous. We have uncovered considerable and sizable frauds: complex money laundering schemes, a narcotics ring, overt sexual harassment, theft of intellectual property, theft and fraud of investor money and trust, spousal abuse, and blatant lies regarding accomplishments.

Our firm conducts global background checks, business intelligence, and corporate investigations. Our clients include lenders, private equity funds, investors, hedge funds, investment advisers, law firms, insurance companies, pension funds, corporations, and government agencies.

Conducting background checks is no longer a cloak-and-dagger operation devised in a dimly lit and smoky room. The need to know more is not only something we preach from our desks but also has become the suggested method of regulators. Background checks are a mandated component of the Sarbanes-Oxley Act, U.S. Patriot Act, Know Your Customer, and corporate governance.

With the help of investigators and intelligence analysts, we conduct exhaustive public record and database research, verifications, and independent interviews on individuals and companies before deals are inked, companies are merged/acquired, or executives are hired. I have spent more than 12 years with the FBI investigating white-collar crime, and my experiences there were not nearly as enlightening as those I have witnessed since I started Corporate Resolutions, Inc. What we have encountered in this business is more than fodder at a cocktail party. The stories are diverse, yet there is one theme common throughout them all: deception.

Recently media such as *The Wall Street Journal*, *The New York Times*, *Hedgeworld*, *Kiplinger's*, CNBC, Bloomberg, and Fox Business Network have sought out our professional expert investigative perspective on the Madoff scandal, Robert Allen Stanford, and Ponzi schemes in general. Our message has always been the same: There is no such thing as too much due diligence. Desktop research is not sufficient. The Madoff scandal was a game-changer for investors. The risk investors assume no longer impacts just your financials; it is also affects your reputation. As shown throughout this book, blind faith and reputation no longer suffice as solid reasons to invest. We hope our experiences illuminate some of the warning signs that should not be overlooked and provide investors with ways they can protect themselves from future problems.

1

Just When You Think You Know Someone

It is 6 a.m. on Friday. Your first week on the job. For the fifth day in a row, you still have to introduce yourself to the sleepy security guards in the lobby of the low-storied building in Greenwich, Connecticut, that now houses your 13 employees. You find your way to your new windowed office and drop your dark brown leather satchel on the ledge—last year's Christmas present from your wife. Accustomed to seeing tall buildings and a famous skyline, you are still not convinced that clusters of small trees count as a "view." You stare out the window for a few idle moments. You swing around in your Aeron chair and glance over at the four Ivy League researchers pounding away at their black keyboards. You summon them to your office. You need an update.

You have spent the last three months convincing the five old-school members of the board of directors that you, a savvy former M&A specialist from New York City, are capable of running this private equity firm—the same firm that over the past four years has earned the reputation of successfully turning around troubled companies and securing investor money. Now you have your chance. With $15 million cash in your hand, you are tasked with selecting the next investment.

For the past week, your research team has spent countless hours focusing on target companies. When they rush to your office, eager to please the new boss, they show you the balance sheet of a struggling Midwestern plastics business that lacks the necessary funds to take the company to the next level. Two days later, you fly out there and meet the owner of the business. You like his enthusiasm. You walk through the facilities and meet a few of the 57 employees whose jobs you intend to save. Back in Connecticut, you do some legal due diligence and run some financial models. Over the course of six months, you get to know the owner, his employees, and the way the company operates; you like what you see.

You decide you want to acquire the company and prepare a term sheet. The thought of screwing up your first investment makes your palms sweat, so you decide to do a little more homework before you ink the deal. You call a private investigations firm like ours to check out the owner of the company.

One week later, we call you back. The owner of the company has, well, an interesting history: He was arrested and convicted on three separate occasions for "exposing himself" at the drive-thru of different local fast-food joints. Given that "wardrobe malfunction" was not an option on the police report, you rethink your decision.

Really?

Yes, really. The story illustrates that no matter how much you spend on legal and financial due diligence, how many company walk-throughs you endure, scotches you sip together or rounds of golf you play, a person's true character (or lack thereof) is often only unveiled when you run a background check that complements your own research. If a person you are about to invest in is solid, then the information uncovered in a background check will support that. If, however, the person is not who you thought, then you need to know this immediately in order to make sound investment decisions.

The Tactic: Turning Over Neighboring Stones

We found out about the exhibitionist tendencies of the business owner by reviewing criminal records in the areas where the owner lived and worked. Trouble is not confined to a person's hometown. You must consider where the person lives, works, and travels. The criminal matters filed against the pants-dropping executive were filed in a different state than where the executive resided. We always review criminal records and court records in multiple jurisdictions to make sure that if there is something to be found, we will find it.

If It's Criminal, Then It's Relevant

To the investor who thinks a person's extracurricular activities are irrelevant to the deal as long as the person produces or performs: Consider what your limited partners or co-investors would think of that philosophy in light of the case just described.

Moving Forward

You never *really* know the person who is responsible for your money. What's important is to be comfortable with his or her character. We all have different definitions of ethics, morals, and success. You need to confirm that the person who has access to your money meets your expectations, and background checks are an integral component of the process.

Whether for individual investments, acquisitions, or new hires, your due diligence process should, at the outset, include conducting an exhaustive background check. From that point forward, we also recommend incorporating the following

1. ***Dig deeper.*** If the background check uncovers any civil or criminal cases or bankruptcy filings, you should always review the documents filed in these matters. The same goes for any regulatory actions that have been taken against the company or person(s). Taking a look at these public records allows you to find out what the issue was and see the person's demeanor during the situation. If a person were accused of wrongdoing, did he or she embrace a Mel Gibson-esque attitude, or did the person cooperate with attorneys, law enforcement, and/or regulators? How did the matter get resolved? The answers to these questions may surprise you. Talk to independent third parties to confirm how it was resolved to make sure the matter will not become your problem in the future. If the problem happens again, you can explain to your board of directors, limited partners, co-investors, or others that you did everything to address the issue. You will not be subject to redress for being eager; you will, however, for being lazy.

2. ***Interview managers/management.*** If you find a person has been involved in any controversies, compromising reputational issues, or inflammatory lawsuits, or there were factual discrepancies on his resume, talk to the person. Document his statements so you have it in the file and on the record, should anything happen down the road. Also, public records only tell a part of the story. If you find an executive was sued for securities fraud, get the executive's side of the story. There may be mitigating circumstances that explain what happened.

3. ***Contact former employees.*** Former employees are constantly overlooked and undervalued in the due diligence process. These people often have enormous amounts of valuable information that will assist you in your deal.

4. ***Ongoing monitoring.*** A background check should not be considered finite. Conduct annual or biennial background checks, get daily news alerts, and monitor relevant blogs. Stay on top of

your investment. Just because someone met your investment standards at the beginning does not necessarily mean they will stay true to your expectations.

5. ***Consider a whistleblower hotline.*** Many investors do not realize how easy it is to implement an anonymous tip line. It is an inexpensive preventive type of insurance where you offer employees, vendors, and others a vehicle to anonymously report not only fraud and unethical behavior but also unsafe work conditions, violence in the workplace, drug use, and so on. There are no downsides to the hotline; it is a win-win for employees, investors, board members, and regulators.

2

A Swindler State of Mind

Many people will fudge a little bit on the facts. Was he really the tight end who caught the winning pass in high school, or did he sit on the bench? Did she make Dean's List all four years in college or just get a few A's in English?

This is a big problem. Though by and large, particularly when it comes to money and investing, most people are honest, unprepared investors tend to assume *everyone* is as honest as they are. But you can't spot a fraud unless you think like a liar.

Before we go further, following is a brief primer on a few basics of how to think like a liar—a perspective on the swindler state of mind.

The Idea

You begin with an idea that might provide a high return on an investment. The idea doesn't have to be brilliant. If it seems to bring in enough money, people will believe it. There are three basic premises to the idea:

- You are smarter than anyone else.
- You have a secret formula/bank/country that gushes money.
- You claim to have found a flaw in the market that no one else noticed.

> ### A Drill of Deceit
>
> Play a little parlor game: Try matching the names Madoff, Pang, Stanford, and Ponzi against any of these inherent components of liars. The great established name in the business, Charles Ponzi, turned investments in postage stamp rates into a fortune—for himself. Black box investment strategies based on computer models and numerical systems to play blackjack also fall into these categories. (*We get to details of the schemes orchestrated by Madoff, Pang, and Stanford later in the book.*)

The Payout

As a swindler, the payout is as important to you as the idea. For longevity of scam, you pick smaller but rich payouts (say, 10–12% a year, with no admitted risk). To make a quick killing, pick large returns on a frequent basis. Do not worry about suspicions. People will believe anything if there is enough money in it.

The Scenery

Always have an accountant. When possible, try to find a very small firm either run by relatives or people relatively easy to bribe.

Never discuss investing details. *You* know how this works. Nobody else has to know. If a customer wants to know how the money-making system works, tell her to invest elsewhere. (But if the customer wants to make a killing, then you must assert that the money should be handed over immediately.)

Never answer questions. Most government forms can be sent back with information missing. So far, it seems nobody checks the entries. Most press inquiries can be answered by saying that "to disclose information would be to intrude on privacy" or "to endanger proprietary fiscal matters." You (the swindler) can address most individual inquiries with an enigmatic smile.

Never mention prior arrests, court trials, convictions, or fines. If you (the liar) don't mention it, nobody will ask. If forced to answer any question, always say that there are too many government regulations and financial rules; everyone slips up on some paperwork from time to time. If there are allegations of wrongdoing made by people who used to work for you, simply reiterate that no one can believe "disgruntled former employees who were not quite up to the tasks assigned."

Never criticize others. (You, the liar, are above that.) Your mission is to help people invest in something that has *no risk* and provides a *nice return* on a regular basis. You execute this without asking investors to worry about how the business is doing—it is *always* doing very well (no need to ask!). Also, repeatedly tell investors how well-invested their money is.

Where possible, contribute significant money to political campaigns of congressmen and senators on relevant financial or regulatory committees.

You (the liar) always wear a clean shirt and a sober tie. Being photographed golfing with important people is good (you appear to be working for the benefit of the investors); wearing a sport jacket or a suit without a tie is bad (you appear to be not working). You are *never* photographed in a bathing suit. If your tastes run to high living, live *very* high: many Rolls-Royces; a fleet of yachts; mountain, desert and tropical homes. A business like yours is so strong, you can afford unlimited quantities of the best. On the other hand, if your tastes are quieter, you are perceived to be the shy genius who lives very well but out of the limelight because you are always thinking of how to make money for the investment partners. And always be sure to name-drop any celebrities or politicians you know (no one will have the audacity to confirm your connections).

Always mention how many people are investing with you. If some investors like you, others will follow. More people not only bring in more money, they also bring in more people. Investors have a lineal descent from lemmings and will go where the crowd goes. (*Again, what we call "flock funding"—when investors follow the flock and do not question the legitimacy of the swindler.*)

A bit of last advice for the liar: Try to find an honest banker in a non-extradition country, either for a quick exit or for a place to go after serving some time in an unpleasant state facility.

Now that you have an understanding of the basic principles of the liars, frauds, swindlers, and other miscreants in the business community, you can apply this knowledge to the following chapters.

3

We Call That a Clue

So what does a background check *really* find? We hear that all the time. The answer is: anything.

A typical background check goes through numerous research steps and utilizes hundreds of public record and proprietary sources to collect information. While the Internet and LexisNexis are both bonafide sources of information, you cannot rely on any one source. The key is knowing not only how to effectively gather information but also how to interpret and analyze the facts.

Some common things we find in our research are résumé fraud or exaggerated credentials. While we may have uncovered this hundreds of times, there have also been some publicized examples: the RadioShack CEO who embarrassed the company when it was discovered that he lied about receiving his degrees; the former dean of MIT who claimed she received three degrees but in fact received none; the Notre Dame football coach who resigned five days after he was hired because he lied about his academic and athletic credentials; and the Veritas CFO who resigned after it was discovered he had not received that coveted MBA from Stanford.

Dried Up Dreier

Another recent example of a minor exaggeration on a résumé that led to a major disaster is Marc Dreier. He was a Yale undergrad, got his law degree from Harvard, and worked for several well-known law firms before he started his own practice, Dreier, LLP. The firm, located on Park Avenue in Manhattan, represented high profile clients from celebrities to executives. With this glimmering Rolodex, Dreier offered his clients the exclusive option to buy promissory notes. But what was so special about these notes was that they were fake. Through the ploy of selling these notes, Dreier stole more than $380 million of investors' money. In 2008, Dreier was arrested and charged with multiple counts of fraud, and in January 2009, he was indicted for conspiracy to commit securities fraud and violation of SEC rules, among other charges. His law firm was forced to file for Chapter 11 bankruptcy protection, and Dreier remains behind bars.

We now know that Dreier ran his law firm like no other: He was the only equity partner in the firm, he was the only one who knew all of the details of every case the firm handled, and he was the only one in control of the firm's finances. Dreier reportedly told his employees that he chose to run his firm this way, essentially like a dictatorship, in order to allow his trusting employees to focus on the law.

We also found that Dreier's corporate biography, which was posted on his website and elsewhere, stated he was admitted to the Arizona Bar Association. But the Arizona Bar has no record of ever admitting Marc Dreier. Arizona, like many other states, has a searchable online database to find registered attorneys—and there was no listing for Dreier.

The Situation: Banking With a Binge

Following is an example from our own case history that illustrates why background checks should become a mandatory component in the investment process.

A guy who was supposed to be an investment banking superstar, let's call him Chris Speed, had negotiated several high-profile deals while working for a big-name bank. A private equity firm was eager to woo Speed away from the weary hours of mergers and acquisitions. The private equity firm had met with Speed, offered him everything shy of a $6,000 shower curtain, and was about to put his name on its letterhead before they called us. Within three days, we learned that Speed relied on more than coffee to keep him awake through his deals: He had a troubling affinity for cocaine as well as a court-documented sexual interest in the illegally younger generation. Our client quickly decided they were no longer looking for a superstar.

The Tactic: Dirt In the Documents

Speed's drug and sex problems were uncovered in court documents we found. The interesting thing about Speed was that he managed to keep a stable job and a *clean* criminal record despite his addictions. Yes, Speed had never been arrested for drugs (or anything else). When we reviewed civil records to see whether Speed had been involved in any lawsuits, we found a case filed against him by a member of his family. Lawsuits involving family members often relate to estate disputes or insurance claims. When we looked at all of the documents filed in the case (which, again, are available for public review), we found Speed had given a deposition wherein he admitted to the cocaine problems and his struggles with child pornography. Finding a person has been involved in a lawsuit is only the first step; reviewing the documents filed in these lawsuits often gives you more information than you expected.

The Situation: The Subversive CFO

In the case of Stumped, Inc., a portfolio company fraud, the board of directors of the computer hardware company noticed during a surprise audit that millions of dollars were missing. The board called a meeting with the CFO, Howard Deepart. Deepart, who had been with the company for about a year, excused himself from the meeting to smoke a cigarette. He never came back.

Shocked and nervous, the board called us to find the money and Deepart. While the search for Deepart went on for months, we tracked down the cash in no time. As part of our research into the missing funds, we scoured accounting ledgers, journals, and a multitude of public record sources. We found that Deepart had formed a company called Stumped, LLC—only a minor difference in name from his legitimate employer, Stumped, Inc.

We began to piece together Deepart's scheme: If Stumped, Inc. purchased 100 computers, Deepart would return 50. When the refund check came in for those returned 50, Deepart would take the check and deposit it into the account of "Stumped, LLC," his personal bank account. Because of the nature of the business of Stumped Inc., there was a large amount of turnover of computers, so it was difficult for the auditors to reconcile the inventory at any given time unless the auditors stopped the workflow. The auditors just skipped the inventory count altogether, thus creating an opening for Deepart's fraud.

Your next question would be: How did he get access to the mail to snag the refund checks? Well, Deepart had recently modified the internal postal policy so that he was the *only* one who would open the company mail—not the office manager, as had been the policy before Deepart arrived. He justified this change by saying that he wanted to obtain a better understanding of the mail traffic that came into the company every day.

Deepart assumed, and was right for quite some time, that no one at the bank or within the company would notice the differences. Once we identified the name of the bank account, the appropriate information was passed off to the FBI. The FBI subsequently froze Deepart's bank accounts, and they have been looking for Deepart ever since.

Stumped was missing millions of dollars. But just as important, the company was also missing a policy of checks and balances that could have prevented this disaster. Deepart *knew* the company had no oversight and exploited the gap.

During the course of our research on Deepart and while we were preparing a report to Stumped's insurance company so they could file a fidelity claim, we found plenty of reasons why the board should never have hired him.

When Deepart was hired he had given the board the names of three references. The board never called these references. When we tried to reach the references, we found out that one reference had died years before Deepart took the job; the other was a fictitious name that belonged to no one; and the last reference, when contacted, was shocked that he was on the reference list because he stated he never liked and did not trust Deepart.

Next, Deepart's résumé listed an undergraduate degree that we found he never received and a Certified Public Accountant accomplishment that we determined was another lie. Of course, this information would have been handy *before* the board hired Deepart, but it was a lesson that unfortunately the company learned the hardest way.

The Tactic: Collecting Corporate Records

We found out about the separate company with the similar name through reviewing corporate records, which are available through LexisNexis and other data sources. Some states have websites that allow you to search their corporate record databases (then you are obviously limited to companies filed in that specific state). Delaware and New Jersey do not outsource their corporate documents and, as such, you need to conduct a separate corporate records search in those two states, but both have websites that allow you to search their records.

The Search for Sources

Note from Ken: In 1985, while I was still with the FBI, another agent and I were responsible for introducing the FBI to LexisNexis. With the help of an NYPD detective, I created the Financial Crimes Task Force between the FBI, the United States Secret Service, and the New York Police Department (NYPD). Both of these developments originated from my understanding of the need for information. The task force is a strong marriage that now plays an integral role in fighting financial crime and increasing the strength of government agencies to address these issues. Although, of course, the FBI is a government agency with many levels of bureaucracy, it allows the agents to be entrepreneurial, as the agents have considerable latitude in managing their own investigations. This style is what allowed me to create these enhancements to the bureau.

In the private sector, at Corporate Resolutions, I still am constantly keeping abreast of new sources of information in both the U.S. and abroad. This is what helps keep us in business: staying on top of the latest technology and data sources to ensure the information you get is the most current. If you are doing your own research, be aware of all the different sources that are out there and do not be complacent with one-stop shopping.

To find out whether Deepart was a licensed Certified Public Accountant (CPA), we contacted the accountancy board in the states where Deepart lived and worked. Many states allow you to search online to confirm that someone is a licensed CPA. Other states simply require a phone call to get the same information.

To confirm (or, in Deepart's case, deny) educational credentials, most colleges and universities throughout the country use National Student Clearinghouse, a third party, to manage their records and handle degree verification requests. National Student Clearinghouse has a website, www.studentclearinghouse.org/, and provides information on dates of attendance and degrees received. Some schools, like

Harvard, do not have their records available through this website, and in these instances you must contact the school registrar directly to confirm educational credentials.

"Caveat emptor" is no longer acceptable. The risk involved in every business transaction is so high that there has become an unspoken corporate mandate for information. Investors, board members, employers, investment bankers, investment advisers, and recruiters know that the "buck" now stops everywhere. Background checks are the most reliable way to compile relevant information on a person or company because they tell you where a person has lived and worked; what his or her business interests are/have been; how many times he or she has been involved in civil litigation, criminal cases, or bankruptcy filings; if the person has had any problems with regulatory bodies or been the subject of any controversial or scandalous publicity; whether the person went to college/graduate school (and did he/she lie about it?); and a host of other information. In essence, background checks tell you what you need to know about a person. If someone lied about where they went to school or what degrees they received (as was the case in Deepart), then there is no guarantee that the person will not lie in other professional circumstances. Sometimes the information gathered confirms what you already knew. But other times what is revealed in a background check rescues you from future problems.

4

The Gray Area: Somewhere Between Fraud and Fudging

We are not clairvoyant. What we do know is that past performance is often indicative of future behavior. It sounds so simple, yet it is often overlooked. Knowing an individual's past is a helpful clue. We have found CFO candidates who had filed for personal bankruptcy protection, self-dealing entrepreneurs who insulate themselves to avoid responsibility, and CEOs who attempted an IPO despite the fact that the SEC previously sanctioned them and prohibited them from acting as an officer or director of a publicly traded company. These situations pose inherent problems that can often be resolved through additional avenues of investigation or clarification from a number of sources. Sometimes, however, the problems are not as apparent.

The Situation: A Lazy Loan

A distressed investment firm invested millions of dollars in a West Coast portfolio company, hoping the infusion of cash would allow the business to grow and provide the CEO, Jim Sneaks, with the necessary tools to develop a broader market.

One day, months after the deal was inked, the CFO called a board member in a panic. The CFO had just opened the company ledger and saw a note from Sneaks that read, "I Owe You $25K." The CFO said that Sneaks' travel and expense reports had totaled thousands of

23

dollars for the past few months, but no receipts were provided to document the expenses. Now that the CFO got to thinking, he said, Sneaks was rarely seen at the office anymore. The distressed investors hired us to find out what was going on with Sneaks.

We recommended, and they agreed, that we start out with a background check to learn more about Sneaks. We hoped that would lead us to some relevant information about where he had been spending his time and, evidently, the company cash. In our analysis of property and corporate records, we found Sneaks had purchased a large vacant parcel of property and had also formed a real estate development company.

Our court record research, which included a review of civil and criminal matters, bankruptcies, judgments, and liens filed in the areas where Sneaks had lived and worked, found several judgments and mechanic's liens that had been filed against him in the last year. (Mechanic's liens are typically filed against a property or building as security for payment of services rendered and are most often used when contractors or subcontractors are seeking payment for labor and/or materials.) These judgments remained unpaid. These public record documents suggested that Sneaks was spending money rapidly but not earning it back, and that he was committing time and energy to efforts outside of the office (which could be construed as theft of services).

We sent a former FBI associate to drive by Sneaks' home. In his driveway was a pickup truck that had the name of his development company emblazoned on the side. We then went to the vacant lots we found he had purchased and discovered that residential homes were being developed on these properties.

The former FBI associate followed Sneaks to try to determine what was going on. This surveillance effort found that Sneaks spent his afternoons at a construction site overseeing a sloppy development project on the property he owned. It turned out the development project had hit a few snags and Sneaks ran out of cash in the middle of the project. Sneaks was forced to fire the project manager and assume the role himself.

Navigating Court Records

Court records are searchable by county. Before you embark on your court record searches, you must first know the county that corresponds to the town or city where the person lives and works. New York City is in New York County, New York; Greenwich, Connecticut, is in Fairfield County, Connecticut, and so on. BRB Publications, www.brbpub.com, has an easy-to-use website that allows you to quickly input any town, city, or village in the United States and identify the corresponding county where court records can be searched. Where available, the website also directs you to websites for these courthouses or civil record repositories. Every county in every state has a different system of maintaining civil records, criminal matters, judgments, and liens.

Instead of continuing his role as the devoted CEO, Sneaks was now unsuccessfully juggling the positions of developer, investor, and project manager. When we relayed our findings to our client, they diplomatically approached Sneaks, lent him the necessary cash to finish the construction project, and told him to get back to work where he belonged. To this day, things have moved smoothly: Sneaks returned his focus to the company, and the company continued to prosper.

The Tactic: Don't Be Complacent

We found Sneaks' distraction through our review of property records. Property records and sometimes mortgage records are accessible through LexisNexis, Westlaw, and other sources. Because these records may not always be current, you can always call the local tax assessor to find out who owns a property, the size of the lot, and whether there have been improvements to the land.

Assuming you already conduct background checks before you make an investment (just humor us), the situation with Sneaks shows the need to conduct updated checks. Sneaks may have been an ideal

CEO before he received funding from my client, but the cash infusion caused him to have a wandering eye. Conducting annual or biennial background checks on the individuals with whom you have invested is another way to keep yourself acutely aware of what is going on. Everyone's circumstance changes; you need to know whether your CEO, hedge fund manager, or borrower has recently been sued by an investor, was pulled over for a DUI, filed for divorce, formed an LLC, or anything else that may indicate a conflict of interest for you.

Not all situations have ended as amicably, as in the case with Sneaks.

The Situation: A Degree of Arrogance

A private investor was looking to make a substantial investment in a hedge fund and hired us to look into the hedge fund manager. Several business associates had referred our client to the hedge fund manager, Henry Arrowgant. We began our research on Mr. Arrowgant and confirmed he received his undergraduate degree from Cornell and his MBA and JD from Harvard. We learned he had practiced law in New York City for a few years and then moved to Massachusetts with his wife and kids and got involved in finance. After Arrowgant worked for a small investment bank in Boston and then a private equity firm, he decided to go out on his own. Within the first two years of starting his fund, Arrowgant surprised himself and his clients with the fantastic returns he was bringing in.

On the professional end, Arrowgant's past seemed unobstructed. But when we conducted on-site court record research on Arrowgant (records that were not available online), the information we unearthed told quite a different story. The multiple DWI violations identified for him were not as jarring as Arrowgant's antics while he and his wife were going through a separation.

One morning, Mr. and Mrs. Arrowgant got into a heated argument, and the police showed up at their house. Arrowgant's wife told the police that Arrowgant had abused her and threatened to cut her up into little pieces. (Yes, that is exactly what he threatened to do.) Mrs. Arrowgant filed a restraining order against him, and the cops told the two to cool down and keep away from each other for a while.

Five hours later, while the police officers were back at the station, presumably recapping the nonsense that occurred at the palatial Arrowgant estate, in walked Arrowgant. Well, in *stumbled* Arrowgant was more like it. Arrowgant saw the two officers who were at his house earlier in the day and began shouting at them and demanded they give him a ride home. After the officers reminded him of the restrictions of the restraining order, they approached Arrowgant and realized he was stoned on marijuana and had loads of Schedule IV prescription pills in his pocket (for which he did not have a prescription). The police arrested him.

Our client was willing to overlook a difficult divorce or a difficult time in anyone's personal life. What the investor was not willing to excuse, however, was the egregious level of obnoxious entitlement and stupidity that caused Arrowgant, an individual with a Harvard law degree, to walk into a police station and behave in the manner he did. Our client ultimately found a sound, safer spot for his investment.

The Tactic: Canvassing the Cases

One of the critical components in unearthing the information about Arrowgant came down to reviewing court documents. As discussed in other chapters, court documents are available to the public. Assuming the records have not been expunged or sealed (and some states have restrictions on reviewing divorce records), you can go to the courthouse and review available court documents in any civil, criminal, or bankruptcy case on file. Westlaw is also a good spot to check for court records. Westlaw, a competitor to LexisNexis, has amassed an enormous amount of case information from jurisdictions throughout the United States, and often case documents, such as docket sheets and complaints, are immediately available through Westlaw.

Bankruptcy Filings

Bankruptcy petitions are filed on the federal level and can be searched through PACER (*Public Access to Court Electronic Records*). PACER has a website that allows you to search all cases filed on the federal level: civil, criminal, bankruptcy, and appellate cases.

Reviewing court documents gives you an understanding of the charges brought against the defendant(s) and the outcome of a case. Also, given that some people tend to sugar-coat their involvement in lawsuits, reading court documents allows you to get a complete understanding of the severity or frivolity of the claims made in the case. Often, the charges a person pleads guilty to differ from the initial charges in the case, and charges are often plea-bargained down to lesser charges, so reviewing the entire case file is important in order to understand the complete picture of what happened. Court documents also illuminate how a person behaved while engaged in litigation. While the issue may have been frivolous, the way the person handled and responded to the issue is as important as the nature of the case itself.

The absurd situation that Arrowgant got himself into was revealed when we reviewed the criminal records filed against Arrowgant. Criminal records are searchable on the state level, by county or by town, and some states have statewide searches that allow you to find out if a person has been involved in a criminal action in every county in one state. In the situation with Arrowgant, the details in the cases are what gave us and our client the information necessary about his character.

5

Sometimes, You Just Gotta Ask

As we all know, there is often more than one side to any given story. Many inquiries will uncover information that requires more clarification than what can be interpreted from a public record document. Clarification can come from a variety of different sources, and most of the time the clarification is achieved by contacting appropriate individuals. The people we talk to include references, former business associates, vendors or customers, regulatory authorities, attorneys on both sides, former law enforcement officials, or even, when warranted, the subjects themselves. While you can interview the subject yourself, it is often more beneficial when professionals like us conduct the interview and serve as impartial, independent third parties who document the individual's explanation of the facts. The interview also sometimes serves as part of the "reps and warranties" in a contract.

Interviewing people is a critical component of what we do. Interviews elicit information that goes beyond information developed in the public domain. As a former FBI agent and expert in the field of intelligence, I (Ken) can tell you that the personal gestures and behaviors of the interviewee are as telling as the information spoken. While in the FBI, I conducted thousands of interviews of criminals and innocent people. As I did in the FBI, you should pay attention to where the person is looking when certain questions are asked; what topics the person avoids or what statements are volunteered; and try to determine if the person is nervous, arrogant, or dismissive. All of these personality traits help paint a more complete portrait of the person with whom you are about to do business. In the FBI and in the private sector, the interviews are always approached and initiated diplomatically and professionally. At Corporate Resolutions, we employ a number of tactics to elicit the most information as possible. No, water-boarding is not one of our tactics. (We discuss details of how to get the most out of an interview in Chapter 9, "Never Too Late: When Problems Arise Post-Investment.)

The Situation: Protecting the Innocent

A fund-of-funds was interested in investing in a mid-size hedge fund in the Southwest and hired us to conduct a background check on the primary hedge fund manager, Steven Freenclear. As with any background check, we reviewed court records in the counties and states where Freenclear had lived and worked. We found he had been divorced for six years and, at the time of the divorce, Freenclear was arrested for assaulting his wife. The details in the court documents were murky. The client had to make a decision: Move forward with Freenclear or move on to another deal.

Board members and members of the investment committee gathered in a crowded conference room to discuss the situation. After presenting the information to the group, they decided to go the democratic route and take a vote: Half of the officers of the firm wanted to back away from the deal, and the other half argued that enough cash had already been committed that it was worth moving ahead. One board member even said, "Life's too short to back a wife beater." With an even split on the table, we offered to talk to Freenclear to hear his side of the story and determine whether he was, in fact, a "wife beater."

As many clients do, the fund-of-funds told Freenclear that Corporate Resolutions needed to interview him to close the loop on some due diligence issues. These interviews have always been an ideal venue for us to act as a buffer for our client and ask the sensitive questions that the client obviously does not feel comfortable broaching with the individual.

So we interviewed him. And no, our first question was not, "Are you still beating your wife?" We asked about his career history and whether he had been involved in any civil litigation. Freenclear immediately disclosed his involvement in an "ugly" divorce. We asked him to elaborate.

Freenclear explained that one night he was arguing with his wife, and when he grabbed his keys to leave, she confronted him, and he pushed her out of his way and walked out the door. He said he knew it was wrong, but he swore it was not assault and was simply a heated moment. According to Freenclear, it was only hours after he left the house that she filed assault charges against him and he was immediately arrested when he returned home later that night. When asked how we could confirm his explanation of the story, he told us to call his ex-wife.

When we called her, the ex-wife corroborated Freenclear's story. She explained that on the night of the incident her attorney had called to discuss an upcoming hearing, and at that time, the ex-wife explained what had happened earlier with Freenclear. Her attorney then advised her to file assault charges with the hopes that it would give her leverage in gaining more alimony. She reiterated that Freenclear had not, in fact, assaulted her. The ex-wife even gave us the name of her attorney at the time and suggested we call her to verify the story. Well, that call did not go as smoothly as the others.

The attorney did not want to talk. She aggressively tried to dismiss the reasons why we had called and stated for privilege purposes she was unable to discuss any of the facts. We told her that because we had permission from her client, we had reason to believe she was knowingly withholding information. We even said we would approach the appropriate bar association to apprise them of the situation. She then said, "OK, OK. Are you tape-recording this conversation?" No, we were not. And with that she essentially admitted that the legal advice she gave to her client (Freenclear's ex-wife) was not the most sound; she supported the story the ex-wife told and also informed us that she had already filed papers to have the arrest record expunged.

The Tactic: Ask And Ye Shall Receive

Sometimes, you just have to ask. In the instance of Freenclear, asking the right questions saved the deal. Our client was thrilled that we were able to resolve the issue and did not rely solely on the documents filed in the divorce case. You cannot always rely on the allegations made in a civil or criminal case. You need to learn more to get the real story.

When we conduct background checks on hedge fund managers and others, our interviews focus on a range of issues that we believe impact the success of your investment. We ask whether the individual is fully vested in the fund. If the fund manager has faith in the fund, then he or she will have personal monies devoted to the fund as well. It is often not a good sign when the fund manager is seeking investors but will not be an investor himself.

Another issue that is often overlooked is health. You need to know that a fund manager or CEO of a portfolio company is in good health and is physically able to perform. When we conduct our interviews, we delicately broach the topic of personal health and, with all of the statements made during the interview, we document what the person says. Of course, we do not ask whether the person flosses twice or day or had a cold in the most recent winter season. Our concerns are whether the person has any health problems that would impede their performance. Also determining whether there is, or will be, a "key man" policy on the individual is another way to address health issues (a key man policy is an insurance policy on a specific officer or employee of a company).

> ### Attention to Accuracy
>
> Note from Ken: From my years as a Special Agent with the FBI, one of the most important things I learned was that all investigations must be conducted exhaustively, meticulously, accurately, and objectively. Because all of the information we gathered would potentially be used as evidence in a court of law, I learned that accuracy is mandatory. Whether the documents are used in a criminal court or, now, used to help a client make a decision about an investment, hire a board member or gain leverage to resolve a problematic issue, the information must be correct. The search for authenticity is an intrinsic component of a background check.

The Situation: Baby Proofed Résumé

We did a background check for a fund-of-funds client that was seeking to invest in a female hedge fund manager. During the course of our research, we identified media articles and Internet postings that stated the manager left her former employer for "health reasons." Some of the sources even referred to the fund manager as having "ill health." But none of these media sources gave specifics about the fund manager's health issues. When we took a closer look at her resume, we realized she had been out of employment for more than two years. Fearful that these health issues would impact her ability to successfully execute her duties at the fund, we asked the client if he was aware of any health problems the fund manager had. Our client did not know anything about the fund manager's health or even the gap in the fund manager's employment history, and so with our client's approval, we talked to her. The fund manager explained she was working at one of the investment banking houses at the time she got pregnant, so she took a leave of absence to have the baby. She jokingly admitted that the "leave of absence" lasted for a year and a half longer than she anticipated, but, in essence, the time she spent out of the financial industry was devoted to raising her child. So the media

articles and Internet postings were exaggerated and raised unnecessary concerns. Our client was relieved that we got to the bottom of
the issue and that there were no real concerns about the fund manager, and his investment in her hedge fund has been successful to
date.

The Tactic: The Friends and Family Plan

Talking to the subject is just one way to get relevant information.
We often identify former employees of a company who also can be
great resources of information. When conducting background
checks, clients routinely reach out to references provided by an individual in order to confirm employment history and to hear what the
references say about the individual. But we all know that references
are usually just a list of friends. Rarely will people give references that
will not be glowing; why would they? Sometimes people provide
names of references *hoping* the references will not be contacted.
(Remember the case of Howard Deepart in Chapter 3, "We Call That
a Clue"? The reference did not even exist.) So we design our research
to identify individuals who have worked with the person being investigated. To achieve this objective, we review lawsuits, comb thousands
of media articles, websites, blogs, and social networking sites, such as
Facebook. We also sift through our internal proprietary databases and
catalog of industry sources. We find people who were not listed as a
reference but did work in the same company or department as the
person being investigated. These former associates often provide
more candid reviews than references. Interviews with these former
colleagues evoke detailed information about an individual that directly
relates to the professional demeanor and reputation of the person we
are investigating. Through these interviews we have found both negative and positive information about a person that was not otherwise
obtained through a background check or just contacting references—
from allegations of drug abuse and abuse of power to detailed
accounts of superb ability to communicate or manage a team.

Bragging Rights

Most people like to brag. Websites that display self-reported information are not only great for keeping up with the whereabouts of your friends but also are another means to identify information about the person you are investing in, lending money, to or hiring. Sites such as LinkedIn and Facebook give details about a person's career history and education that they want other people to know. (Of course, with Facebook and certain other social networking sites, you are restricted by privacy filters set by the account holder.) We often find individuals who have lied about employment or education on these sites or omitted information from their profiles when the information is derogatory. We use these sites to compare the information we developed to the information the person posts to his/her community.

Identifying former employees of a company is also useful when investors are seeking to know more about a company or when distressed investors are buying a company out of bankruptcy. Through a similar process as the one we use for finding former associates (identifying opposing parties to lawsuits, targeted media searches, reviews of blogs and chat rooms, business reports, and other sources), we identify former employees of a specific company and contact them to learn more about the reasons why they left the company and any information about its management team. As discussed in a later chapter, former employees can give critical information when a deal has gone wrong.

When acquiring a company, we always recommend contacting the Equal Employment Opportunity Commission (EEOC) to see if any complaints had been filed against the company or any of its principals. The EEOC is a regulatory authority that enforces equality and monitors corporate discrimination (race, age, sex, and so on). Generally, third parties cannot obtain information from the EEOC, but if you are looking to invest in a company or acquire the company, this information can be obtained by you or your counsel. By learning more about the way a company is run and its internal culture, investors are given information that helps predict the success of the company.

The Situation: Case of Contagious Coercion

An investor hired us to conduct background checks and business intelligence on Rampant, Inc., a service-oriented company that has branches across the country. The investor had heard Rampant was on the verge of a major expansion and hoped to make a sizable investment and reap the benefits of the expansion.

As part of our research, we identified about 25 individuals who we determined had left the company within an eight-month timeframe. Our preliminary research on these former employees found that 20 of them had found work at competitor companies. Because this seemed more than mere coincidence, we approached the investor with the information, and the investor decided to heed our recommendation and told us to begin contacting these former employees to find out what happened.

Our first round of interviews consisted of six female former employees. None of these women were willing to elaborate on the reasons why they left Rampant; they all seemed oddly cagey about their former employer. Finally, one woman explained she could not speak with us "as per the agreement" she reached with the company but suggested we speak with Joan Leader, another former employee. When we contacted Leader, she was quite fired up. Leader told us that Rampant was run by a misogynist management team and that the women at Rampant were either harassed or deliberately not promoted. Leader said the other female employees who left Rampant were bullied into signing an agreement that said they would not discuss the specifics of their departure from Rampant, but Leader proudly told us that she refused to sign this agreement and left Rampant without the requisite financial departure package.

Leader's comments had to be taken seriously. However, we also had to consider that Leader could have her own motives to smear the management of Rampart. So we plugged on with our calls to the rest of the former Rampant employees. The more former Rampant employees we spoke with, the more we heard about the widespread sexual harassment that occurred at the company. Both men and women told detailed stories of uncomfortable incidents they witnessed that triggered the departures of quality employees. One male former employee stated he could no longer sit in meetings and listen to the CEO overtly and repeatedly proposition a female employee in exchange for a promotion.

Although the former employees never filed any lawsuits against Rampant, several of the women stated they did file EEOC complaints and/or complaints with the human resources department, and other women stated they did not want to deal with the hassle, embarrassment, exposure, and cost of filing lawsuits against Rampant.

When we presented this information to our client, he was aghast. The investor knew he did not want to be around when a former employee finally did file a major sexual harassment lawsuit, so the investor walked away. To him, the potential returns were not worth the risk of embarrassment and exposure that came along with the investment.

The Tactic: Secrets of Former Employees

As you have seen in the cases described here, the benefit of talking to the subjects, former employees, and other relevant parties plays a critical role in gaining clarity on a complicated or sensitive issue. Sometimes our investigations have led to interviews that have challenged the statements made by the person being investigated. Like in the case of Freenclear, these interviews then serve to figure out who is telling the truth and what the *real* story is.

What we had in our pocket that truly allowed us to rescue our clients from an ugly situation was the most underestimated resource: people. Whether they are former employees or current and former business associates, these people are privy to information that is often not included in public record documents. Reaching out to these "sources" can enhance the research you conduct and will often serve to either substantiate what you already know or contradict your previous assumptions. Never underestimate the power of conversation; it often leads to resolving a dilemma.

The Situation: Unearthing the Ugly

A private equity firm hired us to conduct background checks on three principals of a paper manufacturing company in California. Two of the principals, we were told, were longtime friends, and the third, Andrew Shady, was new to the company but had come highly recommended. So we began our research and confirmed all of the necessary information on the two original executives: schools and professional licenses checked out, no court records (civil or criminal cases, bankruptcies, judgments, or liens) for either individual, and no controversial media articles or regulatory infractions were found.

The first step in all of our investigative research efforts is to run what we call "identifiers," or the resources that provide us with an individual's full name (and any possible aliases), abbreviated Social Security number, date of birth, and any current and previous residential addresses. After we ran our identifiers and confirmed Shady's Social Security number and date of birth, we examined his history of residential addresses and noticed there was a gap: For a few years in the early 2000s, Shady had no residence. When we find a person is "missing" a residence for a period of time, it is often an indicator that either the person was sharing a residence with someone else and had not used any credit of any kind during that time (unlikely), had been in the U.S. Armed Services (possibly), or that the person had served time in prison (also possible). We contacted the Federal Bureau of

Synergy of Sources

Note from Ken: The New York office of the FBI was essentially a big bullpen of hundreds of agents who were separated by squads or specialties. This configuration enabled the agents to bounce ideas off of each other, get everyone's perspective on cases, and learn about niche sources. The sources the individual agents maintained were of great value to the FBI (and were separate and apart from the informants used by the bureau). In an effort to efficiently capture these investigative sources from the agents for future investigations, I developed an internal FBI system that collected an agent's personal contacts and compiled the names into a database. (We used to refer to sources who were friends and family as "hip pocket" sources.) This database did not specify the name of the source or the agent with whom the source had a relationship but would only identify the type of industry and/or name of company where the source worked. So if you were an agent working a fraud case on Wall Street, you would access the system and see if someone had a source at a particular firm in the industry. You would then come to me, and I would reach out to the appropriate agent and see if you (the agent) could access that source. This kept the anonymity of both the source and the agent. At the time I left the FBI, it was evolving into a tremendous database. We have developed a similar system at Corporate Resolutions with the industry sources we maintain because in the private sector our informants are the former employees, business associates, opposing parties to lawsuits, neighbors, or other individuals that we identify and reach out to in certain investigations (as was the situation with Freenclear). Developing a synergy of sources will reap the most in your search for information.

Prisons and used their inmate locator system to determine if Shady had ever been incarcerated in a federal prison. We plugged in Shady's Social Security number, and the records that came back showed Shady had spent several years in prison for child abuse. We then checked the California Sex Offender Registry. According to what is known as "Megan's Law," a person who has been convicted of a sex crime must register as a "sex offender" with the state in which they live. Each state then maintains records of these sex offenders, and anyone can search their respective state sex offender registry to identify and locate known sex offenders. When we searched in California, Shady's name popped up. Yikes.

We talked to the client and told him what was going on. At this point, we had found the original criminal case that charged Shady with child abuse and ordered copies of all documents on file in the case. We advised the client that there *may* be two sides to the story, and it would be best for us to interview Shady and hear what he had to say about it. The client agreed.

At first, in our interview of Shady, we asked him if he had ever been involved in any criminal cases. "Not that I recall," he said. Then we specifically asked him about the child abuse case. "Oh that?" Shady said. "I was wrongly accused. That whole thing was blown out of proportion." OK, we said, then explain to us what happened. And Shady embarked on a convoluted story that was difficult to follow and difficult to listen to because of the vile nature of it, but the key statements included: "She climbed into bed with *me*, not the other way around, OK?" "That lawyer had it out for me; I am convinced the bitch messed with the evidence." "See, the whole thing was just an exaggeration."

Now what?

We documented Shady's responses and sent them over to the client. The client was disgusted. We then suggested we get another professional perspective of the situation and recommended talking to the Assistant United States Attorney (AUSA) involved in the case to hear what she had to say. The client agreed. We found out the AUSA who handled Shady's case was no longer in the U.S. Attorney's office, and we could not find her working in any professional capacity. We were able to locate her at her home and explained we were looking for public record information regarding Shady.

"That case horrified me," the AUSA said. "After Shady, I quit my job. The details of what this poor little girl suffered through and how sick Shady was...the case haunted me." So he was not wrongfully accused? "ABSOLUTELY NOT!" she shouted. When we hung up with her, the court documents had arrived. We read about all of the details that the AUSA referenced. It was difficult to read. In the end, the client told the two founders of the company that if they wanted investor money of any kind at any point, they would need to get rid of Shady. And they did. And the deal went through.

The Tactic: Corralling the Criminals

In the case of Andrew Shady, we used the Federal Bureau of Prisons' inmate locator system to confirm Shady had served time. The Federal Bureau of Prisons website allows you to search by a person's name to determine if he or she has served time in a federal penitentiary. The system will give you details about the person's sentence, such as the length of time served and the release date. The website is located at http://www.bop.gov/iloc2/LocateInmate.jsp. There are similar systems in most states when accessing criminal records.

Another great resource is the sex offender registry. As discussed, most states throughout the country keep a sex offender registry that is available for public review. Some states, such as California, have the information on a website (California's is http://www.meganslaw.ca.gov/), while other states require you to call the appropriate department for information. Every state has varying levels of information available.

6

Crossing Borders: International Investigations

As you well know, more companies are expanding their global presence through acquisitions, outsourcing their operations or opening their own facilities overseas. International due diligence is just as critical as the intelligence you gather in the U.S. Obtaining necessary information overseas cannot be thoroughly executed from a desktop in New York. Several companies in our industry maintain international offices to accommodate the needs of investors.

Access to public records is different in every region across the globe. While the task of conducting due diligence overseas may seem daunting, sometimes simply confirming a company actually exists is half the battle.

The Situation: The Facility That Never Was

A lender hired us to look into a growing company headquartered in the United States. We conducted background checks on the management team and the company and did not identify anything material that would suggest our client should not go through with the deal. When we provided our client with the final report, we asked if there was anything else he knew of or any specific concerns he had about the company. The client mentioned the company had a manufacturing facility in Thailand that the client had not yet visited and gave us the address of the Thailand office. We immediately dispatched our local investigative correspondents in Thailand. These trusted associates initiated inquiries on the company and conducted a drive-by to confirm the physical address and existence of its operations. Days later we received a call from our source in Thailand. The address supplied by the subject company was nothing more than a dilapidated building. There was no Thailand operation; it had closed three years prior. But this did not sink the deal. The information from Thailand gave our client additional leverage, and they were able to renegotiate the terms of the deal.

Conducting inquiries overseas is an essential component in the due diligence process. But what do you do if you are not a lender looking to give money to a company with international offices but rather an investor looking to get involved with a hotshot hedge fund manager who has worked across the globe? In this scenario, or any other instance where your money and reputation are at risk, gathering information in any foreign country is just as critical as it is when you are conducting business on your home territory.

The Situation: The Meandering Hedge Fund Manager

On behalf of a pension fund, an investment adviser was looking into a hedge fund that had recently opened in Hong Kong and asked us to conduct inquiries on the hedge fund manager, Rich Omit. Our client sent us Omit's resume and told us to focus our inquiries in Hong Kong and New York City, as Omit worked for a large investment bank in New York before opening his fund in Hong Kong. We ran our usual comprehensive searches, focusing in New York, and basically just confirmed Omit worked for the bank he said he had, owned a condo in downtown Manhattan, and received undergraduate and graduate degrees from Ivy League schools on the East Coast. We did not find Omit involved in any civil or criminal records, bankruptcy filings, judgments, or liens, and there were no controversial media articles or regulatory actions on file for him with the Securities Exchange Commission (SEC), Financial Industry Regulatory Authority (FINRA), or any other state or federal regulatory body in this country. We forwarded this information to our Hong Kong office, and they began their inquiries. We were able to confirm Omit had recently formed his fund, Omit Advisers, and had secured a few wealthy clients as investors. With the information we had from our Hong Kong office and the research completed in our New York office, we started to compile the report for the client and review and analyze the information we uncovered.

At first glance, it all seemed pretty straightforward: Guy gets his MBA; guy starts working at investment bank; guy becomes successful; and guy sees opportunity in Hong Kong and opens up hedge fund there. A fairly typical tale, right? (You know if the answer were simply "right," the story would not be in this book.)

As we examined Omit's career history, we noticed a gap in his resume from February 2004 through January 2005 (when Omit opened his hedge fund in Hong Kong). Through our network of investigators in Hong Kong, we began conducting discreet inquiries with individuals who knew of Omit and learned that he had spent some time in India before he arrived in Hong Kong. At first we presumed Omit had merely spent a year traveling throughout India. But because we never rely on assumptions, we conducted some research in India. As it turns out, in 2004 Omit was sanctioned by the Securities and Exchange Board of India (SEBI) for insider trading and market manipulation and was banned from trading in India for a period of five years. Omit's decision to move to Hong Kong was now apparent: Immediately after he was sanctioned by SEBI, he picked up and moved to Hong Kong where he hoped to start with a clean slate. To do so, Omit had to amend his resume so that investors would not know about his time in India. Our client did not want to get involved with Omit for all of the obvious reasons, and we have since found several worthy hedge fund managers in Hong Kong with whom our client has invested.

The Situation: Son of Scam

When conducting business with wealthy families in the Middle East, it is customary for the well-known royal families in this region to hire trusted representatives to seek out investment opportunities in the U.S. and elsewhere. Unfortunately, people misrepresent their connections to these families and often have no access to royal funds. Because there is no database that lists "royal scammers," we always rely on our network of investigators and contacts within a specific country to complement the limited public record information available to help decipher the legitimacy of a representative of these families.

A financial institution hired us to check out the background of such an individual. The person, let's call him Son of Scam, told our client that he was extremely interested in making an investment with the financial firm and repeatedly stated he represented a sovereign wealth fund and that his "family" would be willing to pay any amount of money necessary to make the deal happen. When pressed by our client, Son of Scam said he was one of many sons of the king of a reputable family in the Middle East and as such, had direct access to government funds. We reached out to one of our sources in the country and found out that Son of Scam was "at best a very distant relative" of the royal family and had no influence over any investments or financial decisions made by the royal family and was clearly not an integral part of the sovereign wealth fund.

In other similar cases, we found evidence that disproved an individual's claims to be a member of Israel's intelligence agency, Mossad, and, on the flip side, confirmed a person's declaration to be a former agent for Stasi, the security agency for the former East Germany.

The Tactic: International Sources

In the instances just discussed, desktop research only got us so far. When working overseas, it is the network of people you know that will reap more information than the scant public records available in most of these foreign countries. Because many countries outside of the United States have limitations on the amount of information available in the public domain, we rely on our circle of former law enforcement officers and agents to gather information when we are conducting international investigations. Again, it is these human sources that give you the comfort level you need to move forward on your international deals.

As we have stated earlier, the availability of public record information varies in each country. Hong Kong and the United Kingdom are probably the most similar to the United States in terms of access to public record information. When companies are formed in the United States, the corporate records are kept on file with the Secretary of State in the state where the company was formed. Similarly, when companies are formed in the United Kingdom, the corporate records are kept on file with Companies House (the UK's version of a Secretary of State). Companies House records are available through LexisNexis and other sources. When we are conducting an investigation in the United Kingdom, we often rely on Companies House records to identify an individual's corporate affiliations and directorships held in the country and also to gain information on specific companies. On the regulatory side, the UK relies on the Financial Services Authority (FSA), an independent regulatory body that oversees the financial services industry, similarly to FINRA. The FSA is funded by the financial institutions it regulates, and members of FSA are appointed by the UK Treasury. When we are conducting inquiries in the UK, we always check with the FSA to see if a person has had any disciplinary actions or violations brought against them by the FSA. The information the FSA provides is much more elaborate than the information available from FINRA or most other regulatory agencies in the U.S. These records can be searched on the FSA website at www.fsa.gov.uk.

Similarly, the Securities and Futures Commission (SFC) is the regulatory body that monitors the securities and futures markets in Hong Kong. The website, www.sfc.hk, allows you to search for information on individuals and companies that are monitored by this department. The SFC also maintains an "Alert List," which is a searchable database of individuals and companies that have engaged in unlicensed business or other wrongful business practices in Hong Kong. In both the UK and Hong Kong, however, criminal records are *not* publicly available. Despite access to a few sources in the UK, Hong Kong, and several other countries, the information we gather in our international investigations again relies primarily on our network of sources in each country where we are conducting an inquiry.

The Foreign Corrupt Practices Act

Corporations with an international presence have had to consider another issue: the renewed effort by the government to enforce the Foreign Corrupt Practices Act (FCPA) of 1977. The FCPA is centered around bribing foreign officials and prohibits companies and individuals engaged in commerce in the United States from bribing foreign officials of any kind to gain favor or secure business relationships. The Department of Justice is responsible for enforcing FCPA provisions. In December 2008, Siemens AG agreed to pay the largest settlement to date for violations of the FCPA. The Department of Justice, the SEC, and other international regulatory bodies charged Siemens and three of its subsidiaries with failing to maintain proper internal controls and violating the anti-bribery rules of the FCPA. The Department of Justice claimed Siemens and certain of its affiliates secured government contracts in various countries through the use of either kickbacks or corrupt payments to government officials. It was also alleged that Siemens deliberately and improperly recorded these payments in its internal accounting books and records. Ultimately, to settle the charges, Siemens agreed to pay a total of $1.6 billion, $800 million of which went to the SEC. This is the largest fine ever paid by a company for violations of the FCPA. More recently, in January 2010, UTStarcom, Inc. was charged by the SEC with violating the FCPA. UTStarcom's Chinese subsidiary had allegedly engaged in outrageous bribes to Chinese officials. UTStarcom agreed to pay a $1.5 million penalty to settle the case.

FCPA Explained

If you would like a complete understanding of the FCPA and the ways it impacts you, check out the Department of Justice website that outlines all of the details of the FCPA: http://www.justice.gov/criminal/fraud/fcpa/.

The Situation: Blackmail in Brazil

BryBee Corp., a medium-sized plant in Brazil, had hummed in existence for more than ten years. BryBee was housed in a shabby facility, the type of place where the bathroom stalls made a rest-stop bathroom look opulent. To avoid being shut down, BryBee had an old-school arrangement with Brazilian inspectors: We pay you to keep your mouth shut. For years BryBee paid inspectors to avoid being shut down. Brazilian inspectors would walk through the Bry-Bee building, ignore the state of the facilities, and simply report back to their superiors that the building did not have any overt violations.

Not knowing where the line of ethics existed, BryBee also paid government officials to secure large contracts for it, and had full-time employees marked on the payroll as temporary employees to avoid giving these employees required benefits and paying respective taxes. This situation had worked well for BryBee, and the company had an impressive balance sheet and roster of contracts.

In February 2008, Hindsight Inc., a small U.S.-based firm looking to expand its name and reputation, acquired BryBee. Unaware of the potential risks associated with purchasing an international company, Hindsight Inc. did not conduct rigorous due diligence on BryBee and only focused on streamlining the operations and melding the two entities. Yes, the officers of Hindsight had *seen* the BryBee facilities, but they assumed the poor condition of the building was standard operating procedure in Brazil.

By the end of 2008, Hindsight's group of well-schooled auditors reviewed the year-end financials. After they examined the payroll and both the accounts payable and receivables and felt they had a handle on the situation, they began to take their first look at BryBee. It was at this moment that the Hindsight auditors became aware of the payments made to government officials and that the temporary employees were not paid full benefits. The auditors realized that BryBee may have higher costs for Hindsight than was originally determined. Soon enough, the auditors and the board of Hindsight were in the midst of a problem.

The Tactic: Changes in Brazilian Business

First, Hindsight needed to address BryBee's practices. BryBee was accustomed to operating on the sly, and so the issue of no longer making payments to government officials had to be communicated to the employees and the government officials themselves. We assisted Hindsight in drafting a compliance program and ethics policy for all Hindsight employees, including those at the BryBee facility. Through our liaison in Latin America, Hindsight recruited a compliance officer for the firm who was put in charge of monitoring the operations at BryBee. It was explained to the BryBee employees that because they are now part of a U.S.-based company, their rules have changed: No more gift-giving to government officials, vendors, or others. Once the employees underwent a compliance class on the new house rules, each employee was required to sign a compliance agreement and code of ethics policy.

Next, Hindsight had to address the condition of the BryBee facility. Was the building in violation? How much would it cost to bring the facility up to code? A review of the inspectors' reports regarding the plant failed to show any deficiencies (because of the payoffs made in previous years). This was helpful because going forward the inspectors could not try to shut down the company for historical deficiencies. We got access to building codes and requirements, and Hindsight spent the necessary money to bring the building up to snuff. Needless to say, this also made the employees happy. While they may have had second guesses about being acquired by the American company (with all of the new rules and policies), the employees felt motivated and encouraged by the improvements Hindsight was willing to make to the facility. The inspectors, on the other hand—well, they were not so thrilled with the changes. We learned that for years, many of the local inspectors had received payments from U.S. companies, and the behavior was more or less accepted as a cost of doing business. Only recently, because of the heightened awareness of the Foreign Corrupt Practices Act, is the practice of accepting bribes no longer tolerated. As such, these inspectors have begun to deal with only the smaller companies and not the multinationals that must abide by the FCPA.

Once you are aware of how to deal with FCPA matters and other risks associated with conducting business overseas, such as flight capital, you realize there are countries outside of the U.S. that are known for criminal activity. Some of these countries remain as harried places for investors, while others are beginning to improve their infrastructure with the hopes of shedding their bad reputations to make themselves more appealing for U.S. interests. Brazil is one of these places.

The business climate in Brazil has since changed for the better. As more companies are expanding their operations and staking claim in the Latin American business market, the corporate climate in Brazil has transformed accordingly. The awareness of an increased corporate presence is apparent, and local business executives and federal authorities in Brazil have been forced to respond to these changes.

Within the last few years, the Brazilian federal police have exposed two instances of fraud that have had substantial ramifications on the multinational corporations involved. In October 2007, the Brazilian authorities arrested 40 people involved in an alleged tax fraud scheme relating to under-pricing imports of Cisco items. The people arrested included some top officers of Cisco. In a similar incident, just a month after the Cisco scandal, in November 2007, Brazilian federal police arrested 19 people for allegedly partaking in a tax fraud scheme that allowed multinational corporations with offices in Brazil to evade government taxes. According to news reports, these companies would launder the money through Swiss and U.S. banks, such as UBS, AIG, and Credit Suisse.

Money laundering has been a severe problem in Brazil. Increasingly, the Brazilian federal police have been focusing on multinational companies in an effort to deter tax fraud and money laundering.

But Brazil is like many other countries: the business climate is evolving. But the evolution is a process and in many countries the landscape is still on shaky ground. To ensure a successful international deal, multinational companies need to know more about their corporate partners before doing business with them. An article in *The Wall Street Journal*, "U.S. Cracks Down on Corporate Bribes," by Dionne Searcey, dated May 26, 2009, discussed the recent increase in prosecutions of alleged violators of the FCPA. The article mentioned both Sun Microsystems and Royal Dutch Shell plc as companies that have been closely watched by the Justice Department, and about 120 other companies are reportedly under investigation to determine whether their international presence has compromised any FCPA provisions. As a result of this revitalized effort, U.S. companies will have to meet the sometimes costly demands of complying with the FCPA. This will require companies to take a closer look at their business practices and relationships with foreign governments and officials, and the individuals who oversee these foreign offices.

Do not be afraid of crossing waters to get information. Not all deals end at our borders. You need to familiarize yourself with the individuals operating your international offices. This includes conducting background checks and implementing appropriate codes of compliance to ensure you are not vulnerable to fraud and are in compliance with FCPA provisions.

7

Digging for Disclosure

In many corporate scandals that received massive media attention between 2000 and 2004, the problems of the executives under investigation were the same: disclosure. Martha Stewart did not *disclose* the reasons for her famous ImClone stock trade. Enron officers did not *disclose* all the details regarding the company's financial status. The investment banking houses were fined for not properly *disclosing* the actions and timing of trades and relationships between the buy and sell sides, or for not *disclosing* the backdating of options granted or subprime mortgages bundled.

In the world of conducting character and integrity background investigations, nondisclosure equals dishonesty, and dishonesty is often a clue to other unethical or inappropriate behavior. Corporate Resolutions, Inc. has performed thousands of inquiries that support this statement. Whether the issues have been blaring, shocking, or routine, we have seen enough to know that one piece of information can truly change the way an investment appears. You have to wonder: If the facts have been misconstrued at the beginning of your business relationship, what makes you think the facts will *not* be tainted down the road when the issue involves your money? If your CEO inflates monthly expense reports, will he behave similarly when reporting numbers to the board?

The Situation: The Empty Suit

Board members of a convenience store chain were looking to expand the company and hired us to look into Richard Front, the youngest member of a three-person team slated to run the growing chain. As the investment in the company was relatively small, our client chose to do a background on only Front as he was the one with check-signing authority.

Initially, we found nothing material on Front. His background was so bare, in fact, it seemed that Front did not even have any real experience that qualified him for much of anything, let alone running the entire operation. After several discussions with the client, we suggested we do a little more digging, and the client agreed it was necessary.

We discovered that Front's father, a member of the team and the person who had committed to investing a lot of money with the company, had been recently released from a federal jail for the sale and distribution of narcotics. We found out the other person involved in the potential growth of the chain was a prison buddy of Front's father who had done time for money laundering.

If two of the investors and principals had a history of money laundering, was this convenience store chain their next target? An easy way for them to launder money? The board members did not want to take that risk and walked away from the deal.

The Whitest Lie Is Always Gray

High-profile executives have staged insurance frauds, hedge fund managers have highlighted Ivy League degrees on a resume when they never received any degrees, and fund analysts have boasted 35% returns on companies that never existed. The smallest brag or the biggest abuse of power can all be indicators of a problem waiting to happen. The convenience store tale described is just one among many.

An institutional investor was looking to get involved in an IPO of a young company. The firm hired us to conduct background checks on the founders of the company: a few guys in their mid-20s.

What they disclosed to the client: They were arrested for smoking pot on a street corner while they were in college.

What we found out: They were running a multi-state marijuana and cocaine drug ring, were criminally indicted on the federal level, and had served five years in prison.

Had our client not known the real story, the firm would have been publicly embarrassed when the backgrounds of these guys were released in SEC filings. Ultimately, our client moved forward with the deal, and the company went public. The founders remain primary shareholders, but they do not serve as officers or directors.

Navigating Through Nicholas Cosmo

Of course, having a criminal background rarely means a deal will go smoothly. Among the fraud scandals that were uncovered in early 2009 was Nicholas J. Cosmo's. Cosmo was arrested and charged with running a $413 million Ponzi scheme through his company, Agape World, Inc. Despite what he had promised investors, Cosmo had been using investor money to fund his own lavish personal lifestyle. What is worse, in addition to using their money to pay for expensive jewelry, limousines, and hotel rooms, he also used investors' money to pay restitution from his 1998 criminal conviction for mail fraud. Like the aftermath of Bernie Madoff, investors were left with nothing but shock, disappointment, and the unfortunate crisis of having to reassess their financial stability. (We discuss Bernie Madoff later in the book.)

When we looked into Cosmo's background we found telling information about him that, had investors done their homework, they would most likely not have agreed to have him manage their savings. In 1998, less than six years before Cosmo started defrauding investors through Agape World, Cosmo was criminally charged with fraud in the U.S. District Court, Eastern District of New York. Cosmo was sentenced to 21 months in prison, 3 years of supervised release, and a host of fines. Because this criminal case was filed at the federal level, the information is easily accessed through PACER (Public Access to Court Electronic Records). PACER allows anyone to view civil records, criminal matters, and bankruptcy filings that have been filed on the federal level in every state throughout the country. PACER's website, http://pacer.psc. uscourts.gov/, allows you to search by individual name, company name, or case number, and oftentimes you can access the docket sheet of the cases filed. In the instance of Cosmo, had you run a basic PACER search before investing with him, you would have not only found the 1998 criminal case, but also a May 1998 bankruptcy proceeding in which Cosmo sought Chapter 7 bankruptcy protection.

Beyond the fundamental PACER search, which clearly gives enough information about Cosmo to send any investor running, we found more negative information about him through our other research efforts. When we took a look at Cosmo's employment history, we noticed he had been employed by Continental Broker-Dealer Corp. in the late 1990s. In 1998, Continental Broker-Dealer Corp. sued Cosmo in Nassau County, New York. When an individual is sued by a former employer, we always recommend looking into the matter to learn more about it. Sometimes these cases are filed as breach-of-contract cases, but then when you review the court documents, you see there is often more to the story.

Our media searches found articles that suggested Cosmo was connected to controversial mafia families. And when we conducted our customary review of national and international regulatory actions, we identified a January 2008 arbitration case filed with FINRA against Nicholas Cosmo that alleged fraud, among other things. Further, in 1999, the NASD censured and fined Nicholas Cosmo $68,209 and then barred Mr. Cosmo from acting in any capacity with an NASD member firm. In this action, the NASD claimed Nicholas Cosmo "replaced a public customer's name on an account transfer form with the name of an account at a member firm over which he had sole control, and attached to the transfer form a letter authorizing the transfer of the customer's account to the firm account he controlled, without the customer's knowledge or consent." The findings also stated that Cosmo provided the customer with false account statements and fictitious trade confirmations.

Cosmo's background cannot be overlooked or minimized. With Cosmo's documented history of fraud that was detected by regulatory agencies, criminal prosecutors, civil litigators, and media reporters, combined with his rumored connections to organized crime, it is no surprise that Cosmo defrauded investors again.

The Tactic: Capturing Criminal Records

As you saw with Nicholas Cosmo, searching criminal records on the state and federal levels can yield pertinent information that will directly impact your investment decisions. Federal-level criminal records can be found using PACER (as specifically described in this chapter and in previous chapters). On the state level, criminal records must be searched in each county where the person has lived and worked. In some states, such as New York, a statewide criminal record search is offered. You must check the state/county you are searching to find out if the records can be searched online or in person.

When information is kept under wraps, it does not always indicate a criminal past. There have been times when an individual hid information in order to protect others or to avoid embarrassment. We have also seen individuals who are compulsive liars and scam artists. Those situations are the most difficult to comprehend.

The Situation: Cocktail Party Perpetrator

Thomas Fikshun was introduced to Jake Walden through a mutual friend. Actually, Walden doesn't really remember which of his friends knew Fikshun first, but Walden was at a cocktail party at a friend's house in Westchester County, New York, when they met. Walden noticed Fikshun because he was the only one at the party whose navy blue blazer was decorated with military stars and not monogrammed cufflinks. As Walden recalls, Fikshun was standing among a group of men, most of them friends of Walden's, telling a story about his daughter's decision to work for "Doctors Without Borders" and describing how difficult it was for him to be so far away from his daughter. Walden's interest was piqued, and he joined in.

That night, Fikshun told several stories that painted an impressive picture: He had gone to an elite liberal arts college and then became a Navy SEAL, and after spending a few years working in London with an investment banking firm, Fikshun returned to New York and started working for a "green" company and was trying to raise money for this firm. Walden, a venture capitalist who also spent years as an investment banker, asked Fikshun to send information about the company and Walden would take a look. That was their first meeting.

A Handcuffed Hello

Note from Ken: On the topic of introductions, there is one introduction I will never forget. I was at a hockey game with my kids, and I saw a familiar face. "Hi. How are you?" I said to the guy. He just looked at me blankly, so I thought I would remind him who I am: "It's Ken Springer, how are you doing?" The guy just stared at me, gave me an awkward smile, and walked away. I realized later it was a guy I had arrested when I was in the FBI.

Three months later, Walden and Fikshun had become friends. They hit golf balls together at the driving range at Chelsea Piers and had dry Grey Goose martinis after work. At that point, Walden had verbally committed to investing money in Fikshun's green venture and agreed to find institutional investors for him. One night, Walden arrived home from work and told his wife of his financial intentions with Fikshun. "You barely know this guy!" Mrs. Walden said. Walden realized his wife was right (as she always is) and called us and asked us to run a background check on Fikshun. Walden did not want to do anything behind Fikshun's back, so Walden asked Fikshun to sign a release form allowing us to review his credit report and confirm other information. Walden explained that if Fikshun wanted investor money for his venture, a background check was inevitable. Fikshun agreed.

We checked with National Student Clearinghouse (the company that maintains school records and verifies attendance and degrees received at colleges and universities throughout the country) to confirm Fikshun's liberal arts education. No record was found.

We submitted a request with the National Archives and Records Administration to confirm Fikshun's honorable discharge as a former Navy SEAL. No record was found.

Also, Fikshun told Walden he was a former partner in a start-up company that closed down because of lack of funding. Yet, when we went to the archived website of this company, we saw a list of all of the former partners in the company, but there was no mention of Fikshun.

Last, we found out that Fikshun was indeed "far away" from his daughter. But the distance was not a result of her magnanimous endeavors with "Doctors Without Borders" but rather a consequence of her being incarcerated for identity theft and serving a seven-year prison term.

Fikshun's entire story was a lie.

Walden was devastated. He could not come to terms with the reality that Fikshun had swindled him. Walden wondered why Fikshun would agree to sign the release form if he knew Walden would eventually find out the real story. It did not make sense. At first, Walden felt he should approach Fikshun. Maybe there was a reason Fikshun lied? But Walden realized he was just a pawn in Fikshun's game and decided it was best to slowly sever ties with him. He explained to Fikshun that the financial commitments he had hoped to give were no longer available, and in no time, Fikshun was gone, and Walden never heard from him again.

Fikshun's lack of disclosure is obviously more egregious than most. But the principle is the same: Without proper disclosure by the investee, the investor cannot make a sound investment decision.

The Tactic: Debunking The Deceit

We debunked the myth of Fikshun by checking with National Student Clearinghouse (which we have discussed in previous chapters) and by confirming his military service (or, rather, his lack of it). When you need to confirm someone has served in the U.S. military and has been honorably discharged from his or her service, you submit a request with the National Archives and Records Administration. The website, www.archives.gov, clearly outlines how to submit a DD Form 214 (the required form to confirm military service) and what information you need to provide to complete the request.

Last, we found Fiskhun had lied about his partnership in a start-up company by checking archived websites on the "Way Back Machine." This website, www.archive.org, allows you to see older versions of websites and the dates the websites were modified. So if someone was an executive at a company and then left the firm, you can check the archived website of that company to see what was said about the executive at the time and also to compare corporate biographies from then to now. Maybe the person *used* to say he was an attorney in

New York but was later disciplined by the bar, and so the bio you see does not mention the attorney's license. Checking archived websites is another tool we use to make sure an individual's background is as consistent and clear as the person claims it to be.

Best Practices

In the mass public discussion of recent Ponzi schemes and financial frauds, the term "disclosure" has gained some publicity. Investors of all sizes need to understand that they are entitled to have access to a firm's processes, operations, and strategies. When information is not disclosed, you have to wonder why. To accommodate the growing number of clients who have become necessarily cautious about future investments, we have developed some best practices that we urge you to follow. In addition to conducting background checks, our recommended steps include the following

- After the background check is complete, interview the manager or executive to document his or her explanation of any discrepancies, involvement in regulatory infractions, pending lawsuits, controversies, and so on that were uncovered in the background investigation.
- Interview former employees of the firm to find out why they left to ensure there are no underlying issues of impropriety.
- Verify the fund manager's net worth and that he or she is invested in the firm. Some of this information can be done pursuant to FINRA Rule 3050 or NYSE Rule 407.
- Conduct annual or biennial updates on background checks of the management team to ensure no new problems have surfaced.

Got Documents?

As previously stated, if the background uncovers a person's involvement in any lawsuits or regulatory actions, you should obtain copies of all documents filed in these matters to learn more about what transpired.

- Interview employees if/when they leave the firm.
- Continuously monitor the company and executives. This means monitoring chat rooms, blogs, media sources, regulatory filings, and court records to stay on top of any information that is released or discussed about the firm or its management team.
- Conduct limited scope background checks on all employees of the firm, especially those who are responsible for making investment decisions and/or financial decisions.
- Interview prime brokers, accountants, fund administrators, and attorneys to verify relationships and statements.
- Implement an Ethics Hotline (discussed in a later chapter).

Like a babysitter, you need to stay on top of the people who control your funds. These steps will give you awareness of who is managing your money and will alert you to any problems along the way so you can properly avert a disaster, such as fraud.

8

The Competitive Edge

Investigative research can be a powerful tool that serves a variety of needs. In addition to providing information before a deal is done or resolving an issue after a problem has surfaced, investigative research is also a form of competitive intelligence. While the objective is slightly different, the same resources and creative approaches are applied when seeking to learn more about a competitor or company in which you have an interest.

On many occasions, we have worked with activist hedge funds and investors who hear industry rumors about a company and need to know the legitimacy of the rumor. Activist hedge funds are known for buying a large stake in a publicly traded company, thus giving the activist fund a voice with the management and operations of the firm. Therefore, any major changes within the public company would impact the activist fund's returns, and so the activist fund needs to stay on top of the company's activities. Is bankruptcy imminent? Will the CEO be ousted? Is the company under investigation by a regulatory authority? Essentially, activists need to know what is going on at the firm that may affect the sustainability of the company or the wallets of the shareholders.

The Situation: The Backdating Bluff

An activist fund heard rumors that one of its investments, Handoutz Corp., was involved in the backdating of company options.

Backdating options is a practice where a public company allows a stock-holder to buy options in the company at an earlier date, presumably a time when the stock was at a lower price, thus allowing the shares to increase in value (grant date of options is backdated so exercise price is lower). If an executive has options dated April 3, 2004, when a company is trading at 45, backdating options allows the executive to purchase these options when the company is trading at 23, say in January 2004. The executive has just increased the value of his shares because he will have earned money from the 22-point rise in the company's stock price. The practice itself is not necessarily illegal; it is the lack of disclosure in reporting the practice that violates SEC rules.

The activist fund Handoutz Corp. needed to know whether the rumors on the Yahoo! Finance message boards were true: Backdating of options had taken place, the officers had profited, and the share-holders were not apprised of the officers' actions. To properly address the legitimacy of the rumors, we decided we had two initial questions to ask: Did the people making the allegations have any reason to spread false rumors, and had the officers of Handoutz ever been accused of anything similar in the past?

Through analyzing the postings on the message boards, we were able to determine that the rumor had originated months prior from one person, Jane Grudge, who was a former executive of Handoutz. While this was an interesting discovery, we still had not answered our initial questions and knew nothing about whether the backdating of options did actually take place. Because we knew none of the officers allegedly involved in the backdating would confess if confronted, we

The Insiders

The Insider Trading database deals *only* with "insiders" (officers and directors of publicly traded companies) and tracks holdings (shares, options) of publicly traded companies. This database can be accessed at http://research.thomsonib.com/ and is also available through Westlaw.

decided to take a circuitous route to get to the bottom of the situation: We began to look at Handoutz and the history of the company and the management team. We thought *maybe* we would find some information in either the backgrounds of the officers or the operations of the company that would give us a clue.

At first, we focused on the three main C-suite executives (CEO, CFO, and COO). In our review of federal-level civil cases, we found Handoutz and the C-suite execs were sued for sexual discrimination about six months before the rumors had hit the wires. The plaintiff was a woman named Jane Remisse, who lived in northern California and was a former high-level officer of Handoutz. With the approval of our client, we went to California to talk to Ms. Remisse. We knocked on the door and explained that we knew she had sued for sexual harassment but said we were more interested to know if she, as a former high-level employee, had any knowledge about the alleged backdating of options. Ms. Remisse said, "Well, why do you think I sued?" Confused, we asked what she meant, and Ms. Remisse elaborated: "I sued for sexual harassment because all of the boys had their options backdated and I didn't."

And as it turned out, the woman who was spreading the rumors on the message boards, Jane Grudge, was actually the same woman as Jane Remisse (her maiden name was Grudge). With this information, our activist fund client knew that there was indeed some legitimacy to the rumors and adjusted their position in the company accordingly.

The Situation: The Medicaid Fraud Mix

The competitive intelligence we gather does not always reap results of doom-and-gloom. We worked for another activist fund that had a stake in Medikal Mysleed, a public company that was in the healthcare industry. The activist fund manager saw a press release by the Medicaid Fraud Control Unit of the Attorney General's office in a specific state that said Medikal Mysleed was under investigation for Medicaid fraud and stated that the CEO of the company was also named in this investigation. The press release also referenced other states that were investigating Medikal Mysleed for the same reasons. The activist fund manager hired us through counsel to determine exactly what the charges were; where else the company was being investigated; and, essentially, was the alleged Medicaid fraud a systemic problem that bled throughout the company, or was it the cause of just one officer, the CEO?

We began our inquiry by contacting Medicaid Fraud Control Units throughout the country. In some states, we had to submit a request under the Freedom of Information Act (FOIA). FOIA allows anyone to request information from a state or federal government agency. Of course, there are certain rules and situations by which the government agencies can deny your request, but sometimes FOIA requests do elicit relevant information. Between the FOIA requests sent to these state agencies and contacts we have who are former investigators at various fraud units across the country, we started to receive a lot of publicly available information.

By sifting through piles of official documents and stacks of Medicaid rules and regulations, we were able to find a common thread: The allegations made against the company, the *reason* for these investigations, could not have been based on activities undertaken by Medikal Mysleed. Through all of the documents we examined, Medikal Mysleed had abided by the laws. We were perplexed. We went back to our network of former fraud investigators and asked them to reach out to any sources they had at any of the agencies that were investigating Medikal Mysleed. We needed someone to explain what was going on.

We ultimately got in touch with someone who was willing to take the time to explain the way the process worked and why the company was being targeted given that it *appeared* the company was playing by

Your FOIA Escort

To get the most out of your FOIA request, try to focus it on something specific. Government agencies are more inclined to respond to you if you are asking for something that is easy for them to find. So if you ask for "anything and everything," your request will probably not be processed or take a long time to get a response. If you ask for a few specific documents, then the person reviewing the request will know exactly where to send your request, and you will likely receive a response with some useful information.

the rules. Our source said he was familiar with the situation involving Medikal Mysleed and explained that the states had really been investigating the CEO for years and had been unable, thus far, to bring charges against him, so as is common practice, the attorneys general started to look at the company so they would have access to internal corporate documents that would assist them in their broader investigation of the CEO.

So the problems at Medikal Mysleed were in fact *not* prevalent within the company. With this intelligence, our activist fund client decided to rally other investors and board members and urged them to have the CEO ousted in order to save Medikal Mysleed. And that is exactly what happened. Medikal Mysleed is still thriving.

The Tactic: Going Old School

It seems pretty simple, if not possibly outdated, but picking up the phone and doing some tedious legwork of making telephone calls can often lead to some pertinent information. Such was the case with Medikal Mysleed. We spent hours contacting various fraud units throughout the country, and it was the information learned in these calls that led us to our conclusion with Medikal Mysleed. A telephone is obviously something to which every investor has access. Younger researchers tend to think everything is available on the Internet, but picking up the phone and making a live connection with another person can be invaluable.

Also with Medikal Mysleed, we were able to get more information by submitting a FOIA request. The Freedom of Information Act says, in essence, that any person can request access to information from any branch or department of the U.S. government. Of course, the government is not required to respond to all of the requests, but generally, unless the information is sealed, involves national security, or relates to an ongoing investigation, you will usually get some sort of response from the agency to which you submit a FOIA request. Because you never know what you will get, submitting a FOIA request is an easy tool that can sometimes reap relevant information.

In other instances, business intelligence helps companies understand what the competitive marketplace looks like and why, perhaps, sales are decreasing. Many companies go through natural ups and downs; sometimes this is dictated by the economy, and other times it is a result of a change in consumer needs. Other times, however, a new competitor may cause a drop in sales. While new competition is the backbone of our society, it is not always welcome when the newest competitor in your marketplace is *also* someone on your payroll.

The Situation: The Grapple in the Garment Industry

Disdress, a garment company in midtown-Manhattan, called us with concern. Their customers, they said, were inexplicably vanishing. Disdress wanted us to find out if there were new companies operating in the same market and what these companies were offering that caused their clients to switch.

While we were trying to identify any new companies in the garment district, we also asked to see a list of the current sales people at Disdress. We did a little research on these individuals to see if *maybe* someone was living beyond their means and thus might have another income stream and that could just *possibly* be their competition. Well, if we were not right with our hunches, then the story would not be in this book. But the fact that we were right is not as important as how we figured it out.

Patrick Guile, an employee of Disdress, lived in Weehawken, New Jersey. Weehawken residents have an easy commute to New York City, and Patrick Guile rented his apartment there. Living on a mild salary as a salesman of a small garment company, this living situation made sense. What did not make sense, however, was the forest green Jaguar XJ8 he had parked in his lot that sat next to the black BMW 7-series. And, no, Guile did not recently inherit any great sums of money from a dead aunt or any other relative (we checked). Guile was also not funded by a high-profile wife who earned money in her own job, and he did not have parents who supported his expensive habits (we checked). What Guile *did* have was a company formed in Delaware that mimicked Disdress's product.

With the approval of Disdress and its outside counsel, we accessed Guile's deleted emails from his Disdress email address and found an email to a Disdress customer saying, "Please send the commission to my home. I don't want work to find out I'm doing this." (We were able to do this because Disdress had an appropriate computer policy in place that allowed us to review these records.)

We then got the names of some of the Disdress accounts that had since ceased to do business with Disdress. We talked to these clients and asked them what was going on. While a few customers were not willing to talk to us, we were able to find a few former Disdress customers who said Guile told them he was leaving Disdress, which was why the customers agreed to do business with Guile. The customers said they were worried about the state of Disdress and figured if

Guile was leaving and promising to give the customers the same product as they received through Disdress, then there would not be a problem. In essence, Guile was stealing from Disdress and lying to customers about it. Rather than try to prosecute Guile, which might have brought unwanted publicity to Disdress and the situation, Disdress decided to cut a deal with him.

The Tactic: Combing Through Corporate Documents

The key to discovering Patrick Guile's antics rested in our ability to search corporate records. Anytime a company in any state is formed, the respective state keeps the corporate information on file. Some states, such as Delaware, do not require companies to include the names of officers or directors. But the details of the company name and the date the company was formed are always included in every state's corporate record database. LexisNexis has compiled a very comprehensive database of corporate records throughout the country. Other than New Jersey and Delaware, which must be searched separately, LexisNexis is the go-to spot for searching corporate records.

Not for Profit

To confirm a company is registered as a nonprofit entity and thus exempt from tax restrictions, check out Guidestar at http://www2. guidestar.org/.

9

Never Too Late: When Problems Arise Post-Investment

Business intelligence is not only essential before you do a deal but also in the aftermath. We know that background checks are occasionally overlooked. Maybe you skipped the background check because the deal was referred to you and you thought you knew the management team of the company you were acquiring. Priorities of a deal are often focused on the outcome, namely profits. In doing so, some critical steps are neglected. Sometimes you get lucky, and things move smoothly. Other times...not so much. Unfortunately, methodologies to resolve post-acquisition problems are not taught in most MBA programs.

When post-acquisition problems arise, there are many investigative solutions within your reach. As mentioned in previous chapters, talking to former or current employees often reaps more information than you would think.

The Situation: Buy Now, Pay Later

A client of ours purchased Pretendz, a telecommunications company that had revenues of $30 million. The following year after the company was sold, the revenues of that company had dropped 50%. Our client called us in a panic: What happened to the revenues?

After conducting a limited forensic review, we decided it was best to talk to the current employees of Pretendz to see if anyone could explain the reason why the company revenues had fallen. When we contacted the current employees of the company, most of whom were recent hires, everyone seemed equally perplexed by the decrease in numbers. Then we decided to identify some former employees of the company and reached out to them, too. One of these former employees told us what really happened. Apparently, when the Pretendz management team heard rumors the company was being acquired, they had quickly implemented an incentive for new customers: Sign up now and pay full price, but in six months if you stay with Pretendz, your cost will be decreased 50%. The Pretendz management team had misrepresented the company earnings by not disclosing the sweetened customer deal.

The Tactic: Employee Reunion

Of course, there is no master online database that provides you with names of former employees of every company. But the key is to identify relevant people who worked in specific departments or held specific positions at a company who would be privy to information you need. Sometimes we find these former employees through our review of media articles, and other times we find them by screening resume postings.

When we talk to former employees, or conduct interviews of any kind, our goal is not to intimidate or force someone to admit to something; it is rather to give the person an opportunity to tell his or her side of the story. With the information we gather from these interviews, we then take into account personal biases or motives (for example, did the person who spoke negatively about a former boss have an axe to grind for not getting that promotion he or she wanted?). We then verify or debunk the allegations. Only then can we properly assess the gravity of the comments made during an interview and relay to our clients the necessary information.

How to Get the Most from an Interview

As investors, you know how to talk to people about EBITDA, ROI, and strategic initiatives. Conducting interviews of the management team of your potential target companies, hedge fund managers, former employees, references, or employees suspected of misconduct is an acquired skill. As learned in the FBI, there are some critical components and basic rules you can follow when interviewing someone. These include the following

- **Come prepared.**   You should know the answers to *most* of the questions before you ask them. Yes, the interview is designed to give the candidate an opportunity to explain himself. But, wherever possible, you should have a general sense of what the answers *should* be if the candidate tells the truth. One of the goals of the interview is to determine the person's honesty and credibility.

- **Do not be too aggressive or confrontational.**   If you know or suspect the individual has been engaged in bad behavior, phrase your questions so that the person ends up *admitting* guilt. If you start with, "I know you did this," then the person will be on the defensive and less likely to respond. If you find the person is lying about something, do not say: "Liar!" Instead say something like, "Interestingly, we found a person with your name that has a bankruptcy or has been involved in a lawsuit...does that in any way relate to you, or does it jog your memory in regard to something?" You never know what you are going to learn.

- **Start with general questions.**   When you conduct the interview, ask a lot of general questions about a person's work history: what they do, who they work with, when they started, where they were previously, and so on. Do not at first hone in on anything specific. This allows the interviewee to get comfortable with the interviewer and the process of being interviewed and also gives you time to evaluate the interviewee. More importantly, it gets the person talking. In the beginning, we do not get into any of the challenging areas, and then the interviewee does not really know what is considered important. Of course, later on in the interview, we have some control questions where we know the answers.

- **Ask targeted questions.**   If you were confronting the owners of Pretendz, you would ask questions that lead you to the
  answers, such as, "How did you come up with the discount idea
  for your customers?" "When?" and "Why?" as well as "How
  long did you intend for this discount to last?" The answers to
  these questions will yield more questions that will ultimately
  bring you to the answer you are looking for.

- **Follow the answers closely.**   Be a good listener. If someone
  is lying, the story will often have holes in it. You must pay attention to what the person is saying so you can be ready to address
  the false tales and discrepancies. Let the person talk, even if it
  means a few seconds of awkward silence.

- **Tag team.**   Two-person interviews are best. If you know the
  interview is going to be challenging or will broach difficult topics, bring someone with you. One person will ask the questions,
  and the other can take notes and observe the interviewee's
  facial expressions, squinting, twitching, or nervous habits. Both
  interviewers should pay attention to how the interviewee uses
  his hands, looks directly at the interviewer when answering certain questions (or not), overemphasizes certain words, rests his
  elbows on the table to support his face, and so on. Look for a
  number of nuances in someone's demeanor or reactions that
  help guide you in coming to a conclusion about the person
  being interviewed. Sometimes you can see an obvious pattern
  of lying when you just focus on a person's behaviors. You have
  seen the one-way glass in crime shows on television. Although I
  had that in the FBI, I do not have that now. Two-man interviews achieve the same goal as the one-way glass.

- **Leave the door open for follow-up.**   At the end of the
  interview, ask the interviewee if it is okay for you to call
  back/come back with any questions or clarifications should they
  come up. It's not an interrogation; it's an interview. This allows
  you to go back, review and analyze the answers, maybe even
  get some additional information to confirm or deny the person's statements, or deny the person's statements.

The Situation: The Misled Lender

A lender gave a sizable line of credit to Duped, LLC. Months later, Duped filed for bankruptcy. The lender hired us to find out what happened. Again, we relied on former employees. We searched resumes, job postings, and corporate databases to find any employees who previously worked for the bankrupt company. We found a handful of people and located them. At first, the calls we made to former employees were fruitless; we did not develop any new information to explain how or why the company went under. Then we found a former Duped manager. When we asked him if he knew *anything* about how Duped could have possibly ended up in bankruptcy proceedings, the guy laughed and said, "Don't you know?"

Weeks before the deal had closed, Duped officers hired 50 non-English speaking temps and rented a slew of antiquated computers and printers. The temps, who were deliberately hired because of their inability to communicate in English and thus unable to tell the lender what was going on, were merely *acting* as busy employees hard at work, only for the day of the walk-through. What the lender saw: diligent employees and buzzing systems. What the Duped officers knew: a successfully staged operation that would revert to empty offices and meager balance sheets the next day.

Thankfully, our client was able to recover their investment, as they were secured creditors in the bankruptcy proceeding.

Insuring Investments

Whenever fraud or theft is suspected, we recommend our clients immediately notify their insurance companies (this will not cause rates to increase). Most companies have fidelity coverage, and common fidelity insurance policies cover up to $1 million, at a minimum. Once the insurance company is put on notice that you have a possible claim, you are required to get back to them generally within 90 days to let them know the status of the situation. During this time, you are required to commence an investigation into the problem and report back to the insurance company with your findings. (That is where we come in.) If the investigation reveals that misconduct or theft did occur by an officer and you have an investigative report that proves the case, your fidelity insurance will reimburse you accordingly (and often cover the cost of the investigation as well).

In addition, another way to prevent fraud is to monitor your portfolio company's activities because circumstances change. This means conducting biennial background checks on your management team and constantly checking media sources, blogs, and other Internet postings to ensure there is no new potentially damaging information about the company. Staying on top of your portfolio company means more than just inspecting the revenue stream.

Protecting the Innocent

Post-investment research is not always initiated to resolve challenging internal problems. Sometimes after a deal is done, you just want to make sure you understand what transpired, especially when you are involved in distressed investments.

Because rumors spread as fast as California wildfires, this type of research is often crucial when seeking clarity on an issue. We have seen instances where individuals have been wrongfully accused of criminal behavior by authorities or regulators. The news of someone's wrongdoing is front-page material, but the news of a person's innocence is a small-font entry on the back page (if at all).

The Situation: The Faultless Fraud

Derek Legitt, an entrepreneur, was approaching his 75th birthday and decided he wanted to sell his business and retire. A few years before, Legitt was named as a co-defendant in a securities fraud case.

The case gained national attention because the main perpetrator, Nicholas Baddude, caused hundreds of people to lose significant amounts of money. It was alleged in the criminal case and in numerous media reports that Legitt was a co-conspirator in the scheme. While Legitt was never indicted, his name was linked with Baddude, and his reputation had been tarnished. Because of this, Legitt knew that he would have trouble selling his company. So Legitt called us.

Because we are not in the business of public relations, we explained to Legitt that we could not conduct an inquiry directly for him because then people would question the legitimacy and independence of our research. So Legitt hired us through his legal counsel so that we could properly conduct a meticulous investigation designed to figure out what happened in the securities fraud scheme and to determine Legitt's culpability.

We read through the hundreds of media articles that discussed Baddude and found every one of them had connected Legitt to the fraud. When we reviewed the court documents, we found Legitt had been *named* as a defendant in the criminal case, but he was never personally charged with any wrongdoing. We realized the only way to truly resolve the issue was to start talking to people involved in the case. At the outset, we decided it was best to get a formal statement from Legitt about what had happened. If he was truly innocent, then why was he even connected to the scheme? Through a series of interviews with Legitt, he explained he was an officer of a bank where the fraud took place. Baddude had several accounts at Legitt's bank, and because Legitt was an officer of the bank, he was named in the criminal case. Everyone assumed Legitt had to be involved. Legitt repeatedly said he knew of Baddude but had no knowledge of the fraud. To confirm Legitt's statements, we needed to see what Legitt knew and when. We asked him for access to his email accounts (both work and personal), and with the help of his former associates at the bank, we were able to review relevant bank documents and his old email account at the bank.

Our team of investigators spent days organizing this information into two sections: information that *may* have incriminated Legitt and information that exonerated him. In the incriminating pile, we had a series of email messages to and from Baddude about his accounts at the bank. In each message, Legitt made clear assertions and requests for clarification about status and activity. And in every response, Baddude was shifty. This was the only information we uncovered that would have connected Legitt to Baddude.

We then met with the attorneys on both sides of the criminal case, the FBI agents, and prosecutors involved—and even Baddude himself. The meeting with Baddude was entertaining. He was in many ways impressed that he was able to pull off the fraud for as long as he did. He felt the need to tell us about the numerous times he *almost* got caught. Because sitting in a prison and talking to a convict is not the most pleasant of atmospheres, we pressed Baddude about his relationship with Legitt. Baddude simply said, "That poor guy got played." Baddude said Legitt had no idea what Baddude had concocted at Legitt's bank, and while we would not describe Baddude as remorseful about Legitt being implicated in the scheme, Baddude did seem somewhat distressed about it.

The Tactic: Don't Stop Digging

All of our interviews, meetings, and document analysis produced the same result: Legitt was innocent. We compiled all of our efforts and conclusions into a written report for Legitt's attorney. Then, when Legitt was shopping his business, he would tell all of his corporate suitors to discuss the investigation with his attorney. Once the potential buyers read the report, a thorough investigation conducted by an independent third-party, they would have comfort in knowing they were not buying a business from a dishonest man. And if questions arose in the future, our report would show the matter was properly vetted. Ultimately, Legitt successfully sold his business.

In Legitt's situation, the research went beyond what could be found in the public domain. The information unearthed was necessary for Legitt to continue his professional endeavors without feeling as if he had a misplaced scarlet letter on his head.

Never take information on face value alone. As illustrated in the stories of Legitt, Duped, and Pretendz, the extra steps you take to uncover the truth directly impact the success of your deal.

10

Tracking Down a Threat

It was lunchtime on a Friday at FormChem, a bustling chemical company on the West Coast. Scientists and engineers crowded into the cafeteria for their daily ingestion of sandwiches and pizza. The CEO of FormChem, Jim NoKloo, decided to pop into the cafeteria and chat with his employees. As he left one table and headed for another, his BlackBerry buzzed. He saw an email that read, "If you do not follow my instructions, I will steal the company formulas and take down your operation completely."

At first NoKloo thought it was a joke or some deranged form of spam. Later that day, he received another email on his BlackBerry with an equally threatening statement. NoKloo quickly returned to his office and re-read the emails. Who could have sent these? Were these threats legitimate? If any of his clients, all major players in the biotech industry, got wind of this threat, he would lose his business. As his mind raced, he called the general counsel of his firm, who in turn called us.

With a team of computer forensic experts, we traveled to Form-Chem's offices. The email *appeared* to have been sent from the account of an employee who no longer worked for FormChem. We were quickly able to determine that the sender of the threats must have been someone who *currently* worked for the company, and was in FormChem offices or was on its network at the time the email was sent. To avoid any disruption at FormChem and to ensure the threats were not leaked to the press, remote access to the network was suspended, and our team imaged company computers after the offices were closed, when no employees were present. Through imaging certain computers and reviewing employee schedules and referencing the information with employee alibis, we were able to narrow down the list of possible suspects to six individuals, all members of the IT department at FormChem. The next day, we conducted interviews of these six individuals. We gave them "Upjohn" warnings (the civil version of Miranda rights; informs employees they are the subject of an investigation) and asked for their cooperation. Based on the information gleaned from these interviews, we were able to further narrow the list to three possible suspects.

Executives receive anonymous threatening correspondence more often than you would think. Behind every one of these emails or letters is a person with a motive and a desire. The trick is tracking down the origin of the threat.

Our next logical step was to do some fact-gathering on these three members of FormChem's IT department. Information on two of these individuals did not reap anything of substance for the investigation. However, our research on the third suspect, Kevin Axtagrinde, found that his wife, Layla, owned a temp agency that previously had a contract with FormChem to provide data entry employees, most of whom were nondocumented workers. After

Your Computer's Memory Is Better Than Yours

Imaging a computer is when a team of forensic computer experts takes a mirror image "(forensic image)" of the computer's hard drive. This process is designed to withstand scrutiny in a legal proceeding. The forensic experts then retrieve all documents, emails, and pictures from the computer, which can then be reviewed for anything troublesome, potentially damaging, or threatening. Just because you press "delete" on an email or document does not necessarily mean it no longer exists. Unless the computer has written over that document/email (which happens after an extended length of time) or the computer has specific software that does, indeed, delete the text from the hard drive's memory, then the text is not really deleted.

speaking with NoKloo, we learned that FormChem had terminated its relationship with Layla's company. Apparently, FormChem was not happy with her services and refused to pay several invoices totaling in excess of $100,000.

We also found out that Kevin Axtagrinde owned a few rundown apartments near FormChem offices and rented these apartments to the data entry employees who worked for his wife's temp agency.

With money coming to Layla for providing the temporary employees and money coming to Kevin for housing them, for a while the situation had been a win-win for the Axtagrinde household. But now that the FormChem cash flow was stymied for the Axtagrindes, it seemed they had a motive for sending the emails to NoKloo.

Our computer forensics team returned to Kevin's office and imaged his computer. We found that not only did Kevin have an extra hard drive on his computer that was not authorized by the company, but that he had also installed "Trojan software" that was enabling him to access Jim NoKloo's computer without NoKloo's knowledge.

With all of this evidence, it was apparent that Kevin Axtagrinde was the culprit. With the approval of the general counsel for Form-Chem, we approached Kevin and apprised him of the results of our investigation, and he fessed up. In exchange for Kevin's cooperation, FormChem had Kevin sign a document stating he resigned from FormChem, and he agreed not to leak the information to anyone, including the press. In turn, FormChem agreed not to press charges against him. Since Kevin left, things have been operating smoothly, and Jim NoKloo is no longer apprehensive when checking his emails on his BlackBerry.

Detecting a Slumlord

Our review of property records found the buildings owned by Kevin Axtagrinde. We knew these apartments were being rented because we found a few civil eviction lawsuits filed by the landlord, Kevin Axtagrinde, against tenants of his.

The Tactic: Three Principles of Wrongdoing

People responsible for wrongdoing usually have motive, access, and the knowledge to commit the fraud. In this case, Kevin Axtagrinde's motive was that his wife got stiffed for $100,000, he was no longer able to play slumlord to the FormChem temporary workers from her agency, and we later learned Kevin had hoped to be promoted to a senior position, but he never got the promotion. Because of Kevin's role in the company, he had the capacity to tamper with FormChem's internal and external computer systems and could potentially follow through with the threat.

Spyware

Trojan software, also known as spyware, are programs that are surreptitiously installed on someone's computer and monitors the actions on that computer without the owner's knowledge. There are ways to detect and remove spyware on a computer.

You Have an Internal Problem: Now What?

We have found that no matter what the circumstances are, when conducting a proper corporate investigation, it is beneficial to follow some fundamental steps. When trying to find your most logical suspect or figure out "whodunit," consider who had the knowledge, access, and motivation to commit the crime. For these purposes, "knowledge" refers to information or data protected by a company's policies of the information in the email or correspondence. Kevin Axtagrinde had knowledge about the way FormChem's IT department worked and the intricacies of the information held on the company network. "Access" applies to an individual's ability to have a means of entry into a company's physical offices, accounting records, personnel files, or, in the case of Kevin Axtagrinde, a company's computer network. And "motivation" is defined by a person's motive, inclination, or desire to initiate the fraud.

Because identifying the proper suspect can be complex, we always recommend that appropriate outside experts conduct the investigation and be retained through counsel to conduct an independent and thorough investigation. If you handle the situation yourself, you may end up causing more damage to you and your company. For instance, if you wrongfully accuse an employee of wrongdoing, you risk being sued. Always try to assume the employee is innocent until proven otherwise. It is critical to know the facts.

We also strongly urge you to limit your company's exposure to the incident. Be discreet. Try not to tell too many people about the situation and avoid any publicity or media attention. The fewer people involved in the investigation, the better for your company, the morale of the employees, and the sanctity of the evidence. And, last, identify and segregate potential evidence. Even turning on an employee's computer could compromise the evidence. Allow the investigators to determine what is or could be evidence. Do not assume employees can be trusted with the information.

The information gathered in the investigation must stand up to legal scrutiny. You can only do the investigation once—and it must be executed properly.

Another thing to consider when faced with internal problems is that corporate crimes often have accomplices. Yes, some individuals will act alone. But we have found that it is always common for a fraud to have been executed or created by more than one person. In the case of Kevin Axtagrinde, because we expanded the scope of our investigative research to include his wife, Layla, we were able to get the whole picture of what was going on. The accomplice can be someone who works for (or previously worked for) the company, or can be an independent friend or associate of the perpetrator (sometimes someone has unknowingly become an accomplice). When conducting an investigation, you need to examine telephone calls and independent email accounts to see if the person suspected of causing the fraud is having communications with a possible accomplice or an insider who may be feeding confidential information. In all of our research steps, we never limit our work to just the subject's name, and Axtagrinde is just one example why.

Last, do not overlook your information technology (IT) department personnel. When conducting background checks, clients often focus on the executives and do not look at IT, but these people play a critical role in your operation and intrinsically have direct access to all of your proprietary information. The IT guy has the keys to your kingdom: We have seen many instances where IT staff have secretly monitored the emails of CEOs. You need to make sure your IT staff are as reliable as your executives and will not be tempted to use the information they posses to your detriment.

Diploma Mills

We have seen situations where the person in charge of the IT department claims to have a degree in computer science or technology. Yet we have found that these degrees were awarded from either online "schools" or diploma mills. Always make sure the school is an accredited college or university. The website of the U.S. Department of Education, www.ed.gov, has detailed lists of accepted accrediting agencies to contact to verify a school is legitimate.

11

Now That Is Criminal

In previous chapters, we have discussed the importance of clarifying murky information; what you do when the problems are not glaring, but rather nuanced. But what happens when you find something in a person's background that is a blatant problem? We don't just mean a little white lie or an exaggeration—we're now talking about criminal behavior.

The Situation: The Criminal Connection

Sam Surprise headed to the university student center after his anthropology class. Like he does every Wednesday, Sam bought a turkey sandwich and a Mountain Dew and headed to check his mailbox. As he sifted through the letter from his grandmother and the leaflets and advertisements about events at the school lecture hall, he found his bank statement. Because this month, October, was an unusually rowdy month at the bars with his friends (who could resist celebrating Oktoberfest?), he decided to double-check his statement to make sure he had not overdrawn. His eyes widened as his saw his balance: $200,343! There was a $200,000 deposit from Oversight Commerce. "What the hell?" he thought. He quickly gathered his lunch, looked around him to see if anyone was watching and shoved the bank statement in his backpack. He hurried back to his dorm room, shut the door and called his father, Mike Surprise.

Mike and his wife Cynthia were from a low-income neighbor-hood in Maryland. Mike had worked earnestly in a factory for 15 years and had struggled to save money to send Sam to college. Since Sam had left home, Mike and Cynthia had their problems, but had managed to stay afloat. Of course, when Mike got the call from Sam he initially felt overwhelmed with relief. Their money troubles were gone. Maybe Sam was named in someone's will? Maybe Sam had entered a contest and won? Within minutes, Mike's reality sensors kicked in; something wasn't right. He told Sam to keep the money a secret and hung up the phone.

Now Mike was not your average factory worker. Before he had moved to Maryland and married Cynthia, he had gotten caught up in a scandal and spent several years in federal prison for his direct involve-ment in a money-laundering ring with some high school buddies. When Mike was released from prison, he had, as you can imagine, a very challenging time finding a job and an even harder time erasing the reputation he had earned as a convict. After Mike hung up the phone with Sam, the memories of his earlier years were flashing through his mind like a ticker tape. Mike had two choices: Question the origin of the cash or spend it and hope no one would notice. Mike (and Sam) chose the latter.

Three months went by, and at this point Sam was getting rather comfortable with his monthly bank statements. Every month he would receive another $200,000 installment from Oversight Com-merce. And as quickly and randomly as the money came in, so it went. As the Christmas holidays approached, neighbors began to notice that the Surprise family was living quite lavishly. Four days before Christmas, Cynthia Surprise was at home making dinner when she received a call from an investigator: "Hi, I am George Buzzkill-berg, a private investigator working for a financial institution, and I would like to speak with your son, Sam. Is he home?" Cynthia's face froze. In fact, her entire body froze. Cynthia could not get any words out. She hung up the phone. But Mr. Buzzkillberg was persistent. He called two more times that day and three times the next day. Cynthia told Mike about the call, but Mike seemed almost arrogant about it. "Screw the pest," he kept telling Cynthia. Finally, Cynthia's judgment skills got the best of her. She could no longer ignore the calls. She answered one of Mr. Buzzkillberg's calls and told him to meet Sam and Mike at the local diner in 30 minutes and came up with some nonsensical reason to send Sam and Mike to the diner.

Mr. Buzzkillberg knew right away who Mike and Sam were: the two who pulled up to the diner in a black Rolls-Royce Phantom. Mike was dressed in an expensive suit and was wearing multiple gold chains, and when he stepped out of the car, two Doberman Pinschers followed him. Mr. Buzzkillberg approached them.

"You don't have a warrant? Well, then you don't have a conversation," Mike Surprise told Buzzkillberg. Sam stayed silent.

Buzzkillberg leaned into Mike and said, "I believe you of all people can understand how making one mistake as a youth can impact your entire life." Mike looked at his son, looked back at the investigator and said to Sam, "Tell them what you know."

Sam told Buzzkillberg exactly what happened. Sam reiterated that he had no idea where the money came from or why it went to him. Buzzkillberg asked if Sam or Mike knew anyone who worked at Oversight Commerce or had ever done any business with the firm. No and no.

Oversight was aware that money was being fraudulently transferred to the Surprise bank account and had hired Buzzkillberg to figure out who was responsible. Buzzkillberg reported back to his office and spoke to his client, the officers of Oversight Commerce. While Oversight was pleased that Buzzkillberg had dug up some information on Mike Surprise, the leverage that coerced Mike and Sam Surprise to talk, the interview with Sam Surprise did not really shed any light into the investigation.

Buzzkillberg then began looking into the backgrounds of the four people who were responsible for wire transfers at Oversight. While sifting through archived media articles, Buzzkillberg noticed a high school picture of one of the Oversight employees, Ryan Catch. In the picture, Ryan Catch was standing in a high school auditorium with members of his basketball team. The caption read: Ryan Catch and Sam Surprise show off their dunking skills. Ah-ha (as they say)!

Oversight and Buzzkillberg discussed what to do next. Because it appeared Ryan Catch had been engaged in substantial fraudulent wire transfers, Oversight was obligated to contact the authorities. They had no intention of keeping Ryan Catch as an employee. With the help of the authorities, Ryan Catch would not only be arrested but also properly prosecuted, and Oversight could sue and recoup some of the stolen monies. With his client's goal in mind, Buzzkillberg met with agents from the FBI, who told him that they had an interest in Ryan Catch.

At the Oversight offices, Buzzkillberg interviewed Ryan Catch and the three other employees who worked in the wire transfer department. The other three, of course, had no knowledge of the incident. When Buzzkillberg spoke to Catch, Catch denied any awareness of the incident. Every time Buzzkillberg presented Catch with the connection between Catch and Sam Surprise, Catch just repeated, "I know nothing. That is my story and I am sticking to it." Buzzkillberg told Catch he had to make a phone call and excused himself from the room. In walked the FBI agents who had, by this time, gathered enough evidence (in this matter and an unrelated fraud) to arrest Catch. Catch is still serving time in a federal prison. As for Sam and Mike Surprise, they were both brought into the FBI investigation, and the FBI concluded that although Mike Surprise did go to high school with Ryan Catch, neither Mike or Sam had any idea of Catch's scam and were not deemed accomplices by the FBI. Catch has been transferring Oversight monies to random bank accounts, including the Surprises, for no particular reason other than he was able to get away with it.

The Tactic: The Merits of Media

Yes, in this story, I (Ken) am Mr. Buzzkillberg (but I have been called worse). In the story of Sam Surprise and Ryan Catch, we relied on our research skills to find out about Mike Surprise's background (without which Mike Surprise may not have spoken to us) and to make the connection between Ryan Catch and Mike Surprise.

Many people think that a quick Google search or a look at recent media articles will satisfy their due diligence needs. But you need to do a comprehensive search for media articles. We use four different media databases in addition to multiple search engines on the Internet. In doing so, we find articles from the 1960s that can be pertinent to an investigation. In the case of Mike Surprise, it was our media search that identified an old article that made the connection between Mike Surprise and Ryan Catch, the culprit. The major media sources we use are Westlaw (Thomson/Reuters and other publications under that umbrella), Factiva (publications owned by DowJones), Bloomberg (publications with a financial/investment focus), and LexisNexis (almost everything else).

In this case, because Oversight was regulated by state and federal banking departments, the company was obligated to inform law enforcement of the situation with Ryan Catch. Some firms have corporate policies that require them to bring in law enforcement (most companies regulated by state or federal agencies fall into this category), and other companies choose this route in order to send a message to employees that theft and fraud will not be tolerated.

The Situation: Employee Embezzlement

An employee of a corporation confessed that she had stolen money from the company. In her confession to the board of directors, the employee, Penelope Bucks, explained she *only* stole $100,000, but she had since gambled away all of the money she stole. Ms. Bucks expressed remorse to the board and said she would make all efforts possible to repay the money. The corporation, through outside counsel, hired us to determine how Ms. Bucks stole the money (to make sure neither she nor any other employees could repeat the offense), to determine if she acted alone, and to legitimize Ms. Bucks' statements that she only stole $100,000, all of which she claimed she subsequently spent.

This case was rather complex. Because Penelope Bucks had already confessed to embezzling funds, the corporation told her that we were looking into the situation and told her she was to cooperate with us and had decided at the outset that they would not prosecute. Every week we would talk to Ms. Bucks and ask for bank statements from this or that account and then question the origin of certain funds. We employed our own internal intelligence analysts plus a few forensic accountants and a polygraph expert (more on that later).

Penelope Bucks had been at the company for many years and was considered a "trusted" employee. We found deposits made to Ms. Bucks' personal bank account by some of the board members. We had to closely examine each of these relationships to make sure none of the board members were involved in Ms. Bucks' theft. (They were not.)

Because we had a signed release from Ms. Bucks, we were able to review her consumer credit report. When we ran Ms. Bucks' credit report, we found there were inquiries into her credit made by three casinos in Atlantic City: Harrah's, Trump Taj Mahal, and Tropicana. When an individual at a casino seeks to play a game (poker, blackjack, roulette) and use "credit" to play, the casino, with the person's permission, runs a credit report on the individual to make sure that person is able to pay back the casino. Every time an institution looks at a person's credit report, there is an imprint, so to speak, left on the credit report. So when we saw that three casinos had run credit reports on Ms. Bucks, we knew she had gambled at these three places. This confirmed Ms. Bucks' representation that she gambled quite often and helped us narrow down where Ms. Bucks actually gambled.

Every time we reviewed Ms. Bucks' bank statements, we discovered more monies were embezzled than she originally confessed. Week by week, we would continue on our forensic investigation of the bank statements she submitted to us, and every statement she provided led us to ask more questions and for more documents. If she gave us a Wachovia bank statement, we would find deposits made into a Citibank bank account that Ms. Bucks had not disclosed. We would call Ms. Bucks and ask about the Citibank account "oh right...," she would say and then would send us the statements for that account. This happened on several occasions. Ms. Bucks was not a sophisticated embezzler: All of her transactions used a credit card or cash advances.

In the end, once we uncovered every credit card Ms. Bucks had (she had seven) and every bank and brokerage account she had (she had four), we totaled up the amount she embezzled from the company and it was much higher than the $100,000 she admitted to. In the end, we determined Ms. Bucks had actually stolen *one million dollars*.

Through our analysis of Ms. Bucks' bank accounts, we also discovered that she had transferred a lot of money to Dough, a pizzeria owned by her ex-husband. This added another layer of research to the investigation. We did not have access to Dough's bank accounts or to those belonging to her former husband, and as such, we were able to only track money that left Ms. Bucks' bank account. We began to look into the lifestyle of Ms. Bucks' ex-husband and the operations of Dough. In doing so, we reviewed vehicles and boats registered to her ex-husband and found he was driving a Mercedes and a BMW. We also conducted surveillance of Dough to determine whether the pizzeria was always busy (a possible sign of a profitable restaurant) or always slow. We found the latter. We also went to Dough, bought a few pies and charged them to a credit card so we could see what the charge showed up as on our bank statements. This allowed us to connect any line items on Ms. Bucks' credit card statements to purchases made through Dough. From all of our research, we did not find any additional income for Ms. Bucks' ex-husband to justify his ability to purchase two high-end vehicles.

Ms. Bucks also had a teenage daughter with her current husband. We found that during the eight-month timeframe that Ms. Bucks' said she stole the money, her daughter transferred from a public school to a private boarding school. Last, when reviewing the books of the corporation, we found that Penelope Bucks' mother, a 92-year old woman living in a hospice center, was on the company payroll (to the surprise of the board of directors).

With the information we gathered (the private school, the money transfers to Dough, the salary for her mother, and so on), we approached Penelope Bucks. We asked her if she would be willing to take a polygraph examination to determine the veracity of the initial statement she made to the board of directors and the subsequent admissions she made to us during the course of our investigation. We have a relationship with a retired FBI agent who is an expert at administering polygraphs. We called him for this investigation.

Generally, a polygraph exam is not admissible in court, although some states do allow it, depending on the circumstance. Nonetheless, we have found that a polygraph is a tool not to determine one's guilt, but to confirm one's innocence. The rules on administering a polygraph exam are very strict, and there are specific guidelines as to how questions must be asked. The process happens in three phases: First, you have a pre-interview in which the subject signs a consent form and agrees to be polygraphed and is then asked some broad questions (name, date of birth, address) and some specific questions, most of which are used in phase two of the polygraph. This first pre-interview basically gives the person a chance to know what the questions will be and gives the polygrapher a chance to determine whether the subject is capable of taking the polygraph (that is, mentally sound).

The second phase of the polygraph is when the subject is asked a number of control questions (most of which were rehearsed in the pre-interview), and the polygrapher then determines whether there is any deception in the subject's answers to these questions. In the third and final phase, the subject is told how he or she did in the second phase and given the opportunity to explain some of the answers in the second phase (if the person had showed any indication of lying). This last phase is the most important because this is when most people confess to any crimes committed or acts of wrongdoing.

Penelope Bucks completed all three phases of the polygraph exam. In the second phase, our polygrapher found there were instances of deception and, when asked about these instances, Ms. Bucks kept repeating that she acted alone in the embezzlement of the money. She did, ultimately in the third phase of the polygraph, confess to putting her mom on the payroll in order to give her mother healthcare coverage while she was dying in the hospice center. But Ms. Bucks did not alter her story about spending all of the money she stole. When we presented Ms. Bucks with the information about the Dough bank accounts and her ex-husband's affinity for German vehicles, Ms. Bucks then admitted she had initially given him money to keep him quiet because he knew what she had been up to. Ms. Bucks reiterated that since she had gambled all of the money, she had not made any additional payments to him. And when asked about her daughter's private school, Ms. Bucks said she paid for the tuition up front in cash and that was the only way she was able to afford to send her daughter to private school. Ms. Bucks put us in touch with the dean of the school, who confirmed Ms. Bucks paid the full tuition in cash. The polygrapher picked up on these initial deceptions, and it was only during the last round of the polygraph exam that Ms. Bucks confessed to what we already believed to be true.

In the end, our client, the corporation that employed Ms. Bucks, was pleased that the situation had come to an end. They obviously terminated Ms. Bucks, and they had her sign an agreement stating she would pay back the money she stole over a certain number of years. In this instance, while Ms. Bucks did engage in criminal activity, the corporation did not refer the case for criminal prosecution because it did not want to get involved in litigation, risk losing control of the situation, or be the subject of unnecessary and unwanted publicity. The board felt that Ms. Bucks got ahead of herself and was not, by the classic definition, a "criminal."

The Tactic: Combing Credit

We can only review an individual's consumer credit report when we have a signed release from that individual. These are the legal limitations implemented under the Fair Credit Reporting Act. When we have a signed release from the subject, reviewing a consumer credit report allows us to see how many installment/revolving accounts the person maintains and the balances on those accounts. We can also see, as in the case of Penelope Bucks, what other institutions have looked at that person's credit reports. These "inquiries" (as they are called) often tell us a lot about the person's asset structure. With Penelope Bucks, the inquiries from casinos alerted us to her admitted gambling problem.

The Situation: Fraud in Flight

One of our clients was an investor in a start-up airline. The airline, Fraudly Skies, borrowed millions of dollars from investors. As proof of progress and to keep investors informed, Fraudly Skies would provide the investors with tail numbers of the airplanes that had been purchased.

Our investor tried to cash one of the payments received from Fraudly Skies, and the check bounced. The investor called us.

At first, we were simply going to track the tail numbers of the airplanes so the investor could, in the worst case, find or recoup the cost of the planes. The trouble spiraled when we discovered the tail numbers were fictitious and did not correlate to *any* plane.

The FAA Force

The Federal Aviation Administration (FAA) maintains a trove of information about pilots and airplanes. Before a plane hits the sky, the FAA has information about the plane and its pilot(s). We found out about the non-existent airplanes by checking with the FAA.

We started our investigation by running a background inquiry on the owner of Fraudly Skies, a man in his mid-40s named Wally Wicked. Wicked spent the first ten years of his adult life like many other earnest people: He sold encyclopedias. Unlike other salesmen, however, he spent the next five years in a federal penitentiary for wire and mail fraud and theft. Once he served his time and was out on probation, Wicked filed for personal bankruptcy.

But that was all in the past.

Now Wicked was trying to reinvent himself as an honest man with a novel concept: a high-end airline, the Fraudly Skies. Wicked had big dreams for Fraudly Skies. In his private placement memorandum, he boasted of the network Fraudly Skies would rely on to execute its business plan.

The Fraudly Skies network included all of the following (*the italics indicate information we discovered about each of these companies*):

- **DirtSky.** A company that would provide technical support. *This company was owned by Wicked's brother, who had also served time for money laundering.*
- **CrookSky.** A company that would provide Fraudly Skies with flight attendants and pilots. *This company was owned by Wicked.*
- **FugiSky.** A company that would assist in flight scheduling. *This company was owned by Wicked's brother.*
- **ThugSky.** A company that would provide shuttle services to and from the Fraudly Skies' hub airports. *This company was owned by Wicked's best friend—a guy Wicked met while serving time for fraud.*
- **Hooligan & Partners.** The law firm for Fraudly Skies. *Mr. Hooligan, Wicked's attorney, had been sanctioned by the U.S. Office of the Comptroller of the Currency for fraudulent acts in connection with a collapsed savings and loan in Oklahoma and was under criminal investigation at the time the private placement was issued.*

Of course, when an investor first read the private placement documents, there was no indication that Wicked or Fraudly Skies were at all connected to each of these other companies.

As if this convoluted scheme were not enough to keep a criminal busy, Wicked also found the time to pose as a broker-dealer. In this role, Wicked sold corporate notes to investors for fictitious entities (some of which were in this list) and promised investors returns on their monies.

Once we completed our investigation and figured out what Wicked was really up to, our investor client wisely hired an attorney. His counsel fed a lot of our research to regulatory authorities who, we learned, were compiling enough information on Wicked to bring criminal charges against him. There were countless investors who were taken by Wicked: private investors, publicly traded corporations, and well-known financial institutions. Yet, had any of these investors thought to check out Wicked's past, they would have uncovered his previous fraud conviction and his connections to these conflicting companies described in the private placement memo. Ultimately, Wicked was handed one of the largest white-collar sentences at the time: a prison term of more than 29 years. A grand jury found him guilty of conspiracy, mail fraud, wire fraud, money laundering, and tax evasion. Now, that is criminal.

The Tactic: Connecting the Dots

This is really not such a secret, but it needs to be reiterated: Do your analysis. We cannot stress this enough. In all of the stories we discuss throughout this book, the analysis of the data is what enabled us to come to the logical conclusions in each case. Information is worthless when it is in a vacuum. Wally Wicked's antics would have gone unnoticed had we not conducted a thorough analysis of his background and his connections to all of the other companies he had presented in the private placement memo.

A Wall Street Scandal

Note from Ken: When I was in the FBI, I spent many years investigating sophisticated Wall Street-related crimes. In one major scam in the 1980s, our investigation resulted in ten people pleading guilty to their involvement in a $17 million investment scheme. The situation started with an employee on Wall Street who stole money from a dividend expense account at a major financial institution. With a team of more than 30 agents, we spent months gathering facts to identify the perpetrators involved in the crime, which entailed countless interviews, coordinating surveillance, intelligence analysis, forensics reviews, and preparing facts for grand jury and trial preparation. Ultimately, the case resulted in the highest sentence ever for a white-collar criminal case at the time. One of the guilty parties got 15 years in jail.

12

Dial 'F' for Fraud: The Benefits of an Ethics Hotline

Managing your company's risk is a tricky business. Companies and investors try to protect themselves from the mammoth-sized Madoff fraud on one end of the spectrum to more common smaller-scale frauds, such as vendors/subcontractors with ulterior motives; officers who engage in sexual harassment, theft of intellectual property, or embezzlement; and rogue traders who deceive their superiors and breach company policies. Even if you conduct a background check on every employee who walks through your company's doors, how do you know you are not susceptible to some form of fraud?

In 2009, the Association of Certified Fraud Examiners announced the results of a study that said that corporate fraud is on the rise, and a majority of the fraud cases they studied were caused by employee embezzlement. If the fraud is occurring from within, then you need to find a way to identify that internal fraud before it is too late. Whistleblower hotlines are one of many vehicles that companies rely on to help mitigate internal fraud.

The term "whistleblower" has gained some momentum. Companies, both public and private, have been discussing the merits of whistleblower hotlines, and the American Recovery and Reinvestment Act of 2009 includes a provision about whistleblowers. But what are the benefits of a whistleblower hotline? How do companies implement them? And do these hotlines mitigate your exposure to fraud?

The Situation: The Spread of Swindlers

An investor in large retail stores called and said he knew that he was being defrauded, but because of the size of the 100+ retail store operation, he was not sure where the fraud began and where it ended. We then met with the investor and the board of directors and decided to conduct a multi-pronged investigation.

First, we dispatched a fleet of forensic accountants and surveillance experts in the cities where the company maintained stores. These professionals developed intelligence on suspicious in-house managers and outside vendors, and engaged in other investigative and research activities to help identify the root of the problem.

Through these efforts, it was discovered that the fraud was rampant. Our surveillance team discovered that the night before a last minute surprise audit, certain employees would enter the store at midnight and fill the store with all of the required merchandise so that the audit did not reveal any missing items or suspicious activities. And then the employees would remove the merchandise after the audit was completed.

Kickbacks, self-dealing, and misrepresentations were happening in almost every store throughout the chain and also on the corporate level. We decided that the next step in the investigation was to identify the origin of the cancer before it metastasized.

The Tactic: Hotline Help

To solve the problem, we decided to implement an anonymous tipline (available both via telephone and email) in the headquarters and in all of the stores. The CEO explained to the convenience store employees that any concerns, complaints, or frustrations could be voiced, anonymously, through the toll-free number or email address. Within one week, 12 employees called, emailed, and told us various stories of suspicious activities that they had witnessed. Through these employee accounts, we were able to identify and document the sources of the fraud and assist the investors in implementing new corporate policies of checks and balances to prevent further instances of malfeasance.

Prime Time Whistleblowers

This is not the first time anonymous tips have helped bring to light internal corporate dilemmas. We all know the stories of the famed whistleblowers: Sherron Watkins of Enron and Coleen Rowley of the FBI. Yes, in both of these instances the damage was already done, and the whistleblowing was on a larger, highly publicized scale. Nonetheless, many companies and agencies have found anonymous reporting mechanisms to be helpful, especially when they are implemented before an incident.

Most recently in 2008, a whistleblower was the one who came forward and exposed the $3.5 billion Ponzi scheme run by Thomas Petters and Petters Company, Inc. In fact, the whistleblower who outed Petters was one of Petters' most trusted associates. What unraveled was a complicated investigation that resulted in the October 2008 arrest of Thomas Petters. In December 2009, Petters was convicted of 20 counts of mail and wire fraud, conspiracy, and money laundering.

Construction sites have toll-free numbers available so subcontractors can anonymously report wrongdoing. Colleges and universities have blue phones throughout the campus so students can report suspicious activity. Whistleblower hotlines meet the needs of both the employees and the board members when they are properly implemented and serve as a system of checks and balances. This includes maintaining anonymity for all complaints filed through the hotline and ensuring that an independent third party is responsible for receiving and reviewing the complaints. Employees are less likely to report suspicious activities when they feel their names are known and/or they know the person to whom they are reporting the complaint. Further, it is easier for employees to report their complaints to a live person rather than to leave a voicemail message (a fact that is supported by the findings of the Association of Certified Fraud Examiners). When you have an independent third party monitor the hotline, employees are encouraged to speak freely, and there is no suggestion of impropriety. Hotlines should also have multilingual capabilities and be available 24 hours a day, 7 days a week, as most complaints come in after office hours.

In addition to being a preventive measure, whistleblower hotlines also help companies from a public relations perspective. Companies that already have ethics hotlines and code of ethics policies in place are more attractive when being sold because investors view these programs as ideal compliance tools and modern-day suggestion boxes. Also, these hotlines are in compliance with Sarbanes-Oxley. If a hotline is in place and an employee alleges misconduct, such as sexual harassment, then the board of directors and executives of the company have the recourse of asking the employee why these complaints were not called into the hotline and thus question the accuracy of the allegations.

Introducing a whistleblower hotline in the workplace is no longer viewed as a "big brother" move that trumps office morale. Whistleblower hotlines send a message to employees that the executives, investors, and board members care about the professional experience and employee tenure at the company. The hotline fosters an increase in loyalty and a team mentality among company employees. For the investors and board members, the whistleblower hotline provides direct access to the office culture and the daily occurrences of any given company. And, of course, there is that added bonus of preventing fraud, which is often a major incentive.

13

This One Goes Out to the Attorneys

We regularly work with the legal community to assist not only in forensic investigations and imaging computers but also to complement the desktop research typically performed by paralegals. As experts in information retrieval, we are often hired by attorneys who seek to identify an individual's assets; locate witnesses; gather intelligence on potential witnesses or opposing parties to actions; and identify, locate, and interview former employees for predeposition interviews. The information we provide to clients has assisted in leveraging negotiations in arbitration matters and lawsuits.

Our experience is that gathering business intelligence is a key component in developing vital information that has the capacity to change the direction of a legal matter. In one case, a law firm was representing a corporate defendant that was being sued by a former employee who alleged the company owed him money. The firm asked us to conduct additional research on the former employee (the plaintiff) to complement research that had already been conducted inhouse. We discovered that the plaintiff had a pattern of suing former employers: He had filed three federal-level lawsuits within a ten-year timeframe. Our research also found that the plaintiff fabricated his educational credentials and did not disclose two former employments on his original employment application and resume. These material facts, in conjunction with other leads developed during the course of the research, assisted the attorneys representing the company being sued. In these and other instances, we have served to identify information that impugns the legitimacy of a witness's statements.

We have also worked with attorneys to help identify a person's assets. If a law firm represents a bank that is seeking repayment on a loan and the borrower has claimed to be broke, the law firm hires us to see if the borrower is indeed without any assets to repay the loan. (As detailed in Chapter 15, "Show Me the Money: Asset Investigations," the resources for this are plentiful.) Thinking creatively, we use property records, corporate records, judgment and lien indices, U.S. Tax Court records, campaign contributions, and vehicle registrations. And when someone is an officer of a publicly traded company, we use the Insider Trading database to track shares/options owned and sold by the person and more.

The Situation: The Bragging Banker

A law firm called on us to conduct research prior to an arbitration hearing regarding an individual who claimed the investment firm churned his account. The individual initiated the arbitration against the investment firm, alleging the company took advantage of his naïveté and that he suffered significant monetary losses resulting in him living in a deteriorated, uninhabitable apartment.

At the start, through a review of property records and Uniform Commercial Code filings, we determined the individual owned a luxurious home in a well-known building on Fifth Avenue in Manhattan.

Further, to determine the credibility of the individual's statements that he was not knowledgeable about the stock market and had relied solely on the advice of his broker, with the approval of counsel, we conducted a physical surveillance of the individual. That turned out to be the wisest decision: We found the "naïve" individual bragging to a group of men at a bar about his savvy knowledge of the market. The incident was discreetly videotaped, and within a matter of days the arbitration was withdrawn.

NYC Livin'

Many buildings in New York City are cooperatives ("co-ops"). These co-ops are corporations that own a building. When you purchase a co-op apartment, you are not technically purchasing real property; you are instead purchasing shares in a private corporation. If you own a co-op apartment, there is no property record that reflects your ownership. The way we initially determine if someone has a co-op apartment in Manhattan is through a review of Uniform Commercial Code (UCC) filings, which reflect financial relationships. If you have a mortgage on your co-op apartment, then this will most likely be filed as a UCC statement. Condominiums, on the other hand, *are* considered real property (you get a deed when you purchase a condo in New York City), and there are publicly available property records that show ownership, purchase price, contract date, and other details regarding the transaction when you purchased the condominium.

The Situation: A Leg Up for Lawyers

In several instances we have recommended our clients hire us through their outside counsel for privilege purposes. In one of these situations, a group of investors was interested in a German company and hired us through their law firm. As was relayed to us by the investors' attorneys, the investors had met with Herr Hoax, the head of the German firm, and were interested in a new form of media he had developed: bringing the concept of the "Choose Your Own Adventure" books to television. At the end of each segment of a crime-based television show, the viewer would have the ability to choose whether the main character would continue on his adventures, travel to a new city where unknown excitement would be found or, possibly, get double-crossed by another character in the show.

The investors and their attorneys travelled to Germany to watch a few preliminary screenings of the idea and were enthralled. Because of the years he spent in media, Herr Hoax told the investors he had unbridled access to the necessary connections in television who were to assist him in bringing the idea to the United States.

The attorneys had reviewed all of the documents about the company, but for some reason they felt they did not have a handle on Herr Hoax, so they asked us to do some due diligence. We dispatched our in-country sources in Germany, who quickly found Herr Hoax had never been involved in media prior to his current company. What was Herr Hoax involved in? Money. Why did he hide it from the investors? Because Herr Hoax had been prohibited from participating in any investment situation by the German Federal Financial Supervisory Authority (known as BaFin).

Through our sources in Germany and the United Kingdom, we were able to piece together Herr Hoax's history: He was a money manager in the UK until he was charged with tax evasion, at which time he moved his operations to Germany, where he quickly earned the attention of BaFin because of the Ponzi-like scheme he was running there. By the time our investors had met with Herr Hoax, he had already stolen millions of dollars from other investors who were just as excited at the promise of Choose-Your-Own-Hoax. When we relayed the information to the attorneys, we confirmed their suspicions, and they advised their clients to find another investment.

Locating witnesses is another service for which attorneys rely on investigative companies. As licensed private investigators, we have access to information that many law firms and others do not.

If an attorney knows Billy Bystander has information that is critical to a case, but the attorney has no idea where to find Billy Bystander, we tap into our identifier databases and search the country for Billy Bystander. These identifier databases collect information legally from credit reporting sources, telephone directories, and other sources and compile the information into personal profiles. The information we see includes where a person currently lives and previously lived, his date of birth and a limited portion of his Social Security number, as well as other identifying information that varies by state, such as voter registration information and driver history reports.

If Billy Bystander happens to be a common name, we cross-reference the multiple Billy Bystander listings with information we know about him and try to rule out the other Billy Bystanders to make sure we have the right guy. If we find Billy Bystander lives in an apartment in San Francisco but has an unlisted telephone number, we provide the attorney with contact numbers for Billy Bystander's neighbors, if need be, or contact them directly if the attorney prefers. And if our client is an attorney on the opposing side of Billy Bystander and wants to know if there is any information on him that would question his credibility as a witness, then we engage in a background check of Billy Bystander and see what is out there.

As stated earlier, running identifier databases is the first step we take in any investigation. This allows us to locate people like Billy Bystander, and gives us a preliminary sense of where we will conduct our subsequent searches. For instance, if Billy Bystander's identifying information shows he lives in San Francisco but previously lived in Los Angeles, we know immediately that we need to, at least, run court record searches in those two areas. Because the identifier databases provide us with an address history for each person, we use these addresses to find properties owned by a person and companies that may have been formed under a different name but at the person's known addresses.

Whether we are interviewing people before a deposition to learn more about the statements they are prepared to make, gathering intelligence on potential witnesses, or conducting asset searches, the creative research methods we rely on assist attorneys in gaining leverage in cases and arbitrations where information has the power to influence the outcome.

14

The Godfather in the Boardroom

Who can forget the chilling scene in the first installment of the famed *Godfather* movies when the audacious Hollywood producer, Jack Woltz, is sleeping in his gold pajamas in his similarly colored satin sheets on his king-size bed and awakes slipping around in the blood of his beloved, now decapitated, horse. The horse head was sent as a message: Do not mess with Don Corleone. Some of you can probably quote the entire movie trilogy and frequently use the term "going to the mattresses" to refer to getting ready for a fight. Others may have only heard the folklore about the *Godfather* films. No matter what your exposure has been, you certainly know the *Godfather* stories focused on organized crime. The perspective was not that organized crime exists but that it is an intricate, complex *business* that thrives on profit and power, like any other business. But how much of what is portrayed in movies really happens? And if it does happen, what does organized crime have to do with legitimate business operations?

While sparing you an entire lesson on how organized crime came to be and what different factions exist, it is important to distinguish the different types of organized crime. The criminal Italian families from Sicily are known as the "Cosa Nostra," and they operate differently than the Russian organized crime families, who play with a different set of rules than the Albanians, the Mexicans, and so on. The origins of these varying mafias dictate their rules and goals. And for the purposes of this book, we focus on their goals in the corporate community.

In the 1980s, E.F. Hutton, the respectable brokerage firm with
the popular slogan, "When E.F. Hutton talks, people listen," had its
reputation tainted when a branch of the firm became ensnared in a
money laundering scam with the Italian Mafia. Known as "the Pizza
Connection," the Mafia discreetly sold heroin at a small pizza place in
New York. With the cash earned from selling obscene amounts of
heroin, Mafia representatives would carry the cash in luggage and
deposit the money into accounts with E.F. Hutton. E.F. Hutton duti-
fully filled out the requisite banking forms, deposited the money, and
put it into the commodities market, as it would have done for any
other customer. Now that the money was laundered, it was then
transferred to bank accounts in Switzerland that belonged to the
Mafia. Theoretically, because the bank was unaware of the origin of
the money, E.F. Hutton had not committed any crimes. The problem
came when the FBI began to investigate the money transfers and
E.F. Hutton told its Swiss clients that the FBI had begun digging.
This tipped off the Mafia men, who quickly closed their accounts
with the brokerage firm, thus stymying the FBI's efforts to crack
down on the drug trade and money laundering efforts of the Mafia.

When organized crime invades the business community, it is not
always focused on laundering the money it has earned from the drug
trade. For those of you who missed HBO's *The Sopranos* series, the
construction industry is a popular field for organized crime. There
have been many instances of organized crime families infiltrating
construction trades and waste-hauling companies. Some of these
individuals have been federally prosecuted, and others remain in the
marketplace, actively exerting influence. Because not all associates of
organized crime families go by the name Soprano, it is often difficult
for hard-working and earnest construction companies to know when
they are being swindled by organized crime.

The Situation: Crime in Construction

BlindBuilders, a general contractor in New York, was completing work on the renovation of a large commercial space. Blind-Builders was coordinating with its subcontractors and running through the last-minute change orders and finishing touches. Blind-Builders needed to get OC & Company, one of its subcontractors, back on the job site to finish the work, as per the original contract between the two. BlindBuilders called both officers of OC & Company repeatedly. The voicemails went from mild-mannered requests about finishing the job to screaming rants to get the friggin' job done. Neither approach was met with a response. BlindBuilders was under the gun to complete the job in its entirety as per the schedule with the client. One day, the head of BlindBuilders was at the jobsite and had just hung up the phone and left yet another message for OC & Company. Another subcontractor on the job made an off-hand and quiet remark that caught the attention of the CEO. "Good luck with that," the subcontractor said. "Those guys are so connected, you will have better luck getting the President of the United States to finish the job." And with that comment, BlindBuilders called us.

The only information BlindBuilders had about OC & Company were the names of the two owners of the company and a cell phone number. Through reverse phone searches (when you search by a telephone number and find who is listed to that number) and reviewing corporate records, we were able to locate the two individuals and identify them as owners of numerous other construction-related firms in the New York and New Jersey area.

We also ran a search of "Vendex," the questionnaires submitted to the City of New York by all construction firms and other vendors who seek to perform jobs for the city. We found that it was the wives of the owners, and not the owners themselves, who were listed in the Vendex database. Realizing the owners of OC & Company were smart enough to keep their names out of necessary documents, we then ran media searches on all of the companies we found to be affiliated with the owners of OC & Company. We found some articles from the early 1990s that stated these affiliates of OC & Company had employed a known "kingpin" of a Mafia family. Through our review of federal-level criminal records, we found these affiliates had also been criminally indicted for racketeering. The case was brought under the Racketeer Influenced and Corrupt Organizations Act, known as RICO, a common cause of action used when prosecuting members of organized crime. In order to charge someone under RICO, there must be predicate violations; RICO charges must show a pattern of bad behavior.

The problem with all of this information was that none of it directly implicated the two owners of OC & Company, and we found no information that definitively stated the owners were involved with organized crime. We knew the only way to get the answers we needed was to reach out to my (Ken's) network. We met with some friends who are former federal and state investigators, and others who have worked in the construction industry for more than 20 years. There was a consensus among their statements: The owners of OC & Company were, indeed, connected to organized crime but had successfully and craftily avoided prosecution for many years. Understanding the gravity of the situation, BlindBuilders decided to walk away from the $75,000 of work owed to them by OC & Company and hired another subcontractor to complete the job.

The Tactic: The RICO Reason

Media articles helped guide us in the investigation. It was the articles about OC & Company's connections to organized crime that played a part in our research. Because statements made in media articles need to be independently confirmed, we use the information we

CHAPTER 14 • THE GODFATHER IN THE BOARDROOM

find in media and go to another concrete, primary source to either confirm or deny what we found. In the case for BlindBuilders, we luckily confirmed that OC & Company was run by organized crime and saved our client the insurmountable troubles associated with dealing with or being infiltrated by organized crime.

Also we discussed RICO cases and the origin of these types of cases. RICO cases have historically been criminal cases but are now also often used in civil matters. Both the criminal and civil cases are filed on the federal level and can be searched through PACER.

Crime Beyond Construction

It is more than just an ethical issue that forces companies to shy away from dealing with organized crime. It is also the fact that organized crime families have killed or physically injured those who have impeded their efforts. Not every interaction with organized crime ends with a slain horse head in the bed or other gory recapitulations seen in movies and television shows and written about in books. But the reality that members of organized crime do not value life the same way we do is certainly reason enough to walk away from a deal. Shying away from working with companies connected to organized crime is another way of evaluating the cost of doing business.

In the mid- to late 1990s, organized crime infiltrated the stock markets by engaging in what became known as "pump and dump" scams. In these frauds, the price of microcap stocks (penny stocks) are artificially inflated ("pumped") using misleading statements. The pumpers buy a significant amount of shares in these artificially inflated stocks and then sell them to the public at the higher price. Once the perpetrators sell their shares in these stocks ("dump" them), the public is left with almost valueless stocks.

Organized crime played a role in the pump and dump scams by controlling brokerage firms that would buy large blocks of stock in penny stocks, convince (or orchestrate) appropriate marketers and others that the stocks had value, sell the stocks to the public at the inflated price, and then the brokerage firms would dump their shares in the stocks. In many cases, organized crime successfully defrauded investors of millions of dollars. Over the years, the FBI arrested many members of organized crime families for engaging in this type of fraud.

The Situation: The Russian Racket

We have witnessed organized crime manifest itself in the business community, too. An old-school financial institution hired us to run background checks on the Russian owners of a biotech firm who sought a bridge loan from our client. During the course of our background checks, we found very little information on any of the owners. In fact, other than renting property in Brooklyn, New York, we did not find any data to even suggest the owners were involved in the biotech industry or any business at all in the United States. Our client was surprised with our findings and told us the Russian owners had presented themselves as entrepreneurs who had been engaged in businesses of all kinds for many years.

As a former Special Agent with the FBI, I (Ken) have access to a network of thousands of former FBI agents and other investegators across the globe. I made a few calls within this network and explained the situation. One of my former associates at the FBI recalled the names of the Russian owners and informed me that all of the individuals were connected to a known Russian organized crime family. Within seconds, I called my client, who needed no

Craving Crime

If you are interested in organized crime and tracking the whereabouts and updates on Mafia-related news, Gang Land News is a great website for you: www.ganglandnews.com.

further explanation on why the deal was not worth pursuing. Because of the precarious nature of the situation, I assisted our client in devising a strategy to delicately and diplomatically inform the Russians that the bridge loan did not meet their current lending guidelines.

The Situation: Connected

We were working for a broker/dealer who was looking to establish a relationship with a clearing firm (a company that ensures trades and securities are completed within regulatory guidelines) that could generate a lot of money. The broker/dealer hired us to do some basic background checks on the clearing firm and its executives, per the "Know Your Customer" (KYC) guidelines. The U.S. Patriot Act requires financial institutions to do some research on their customers, both existing and potential, to prevent fraud, money laundering, and other white-collar crimes. It was in this vein that the broker/dealer retained us.

The minute we saw the name of the executive of the clearing firm, we knew it sounded familiar. We checked our proprietary internal database and found there were rumors the executive had close ties to organized crime. Because there is no searchable website called Iamamobster.com, the way to substantiate that someone is connected to the mob is through a variety of independent sources.

At first, we reached out to a former agent friend who told us he knew the executive was somehow involved in a criminal lawsuit, but the agent could not remember the details. He told us to contact the prosecutor in the case. The prosecutor was reluctant to speak with us. We explained our objective, told him that, in abidance with Grand Jury Rule 6E, we were not asking for anything other than public record information. The prosecutor finally agreed to help us and sent us on a scavenger hunt. He said, "Go to the courthouse basement, case no. 8712345, box no. 123, find the wiretap transcripts, turn to page 635." In there was a line that said the executive in question was a "made" member of an organized crime family. Suspicion confirmed. Our client decided to find another clearing-house to do its business.

All of these stories illustrate the same point: organized crime is still present and threatens the sanctity of businesses that seek to operate ethically and successfully.

A History of Security

Note from Ken: When I worked white-collar crime in the FBI, I was the agency's representative for the Internal Security Association. This was an organization comprised of security directors from all of the major financial institutions. We would discuss the different types of fraud that the security directors were witnessing on the front lines—this exposure and awareness helped formulate my understanding of the needs of investment firms. Through this position, I learned a lot about Wall Street firms and also developed a one-on-one relationship with many of the security directors. Several of these people subsequently became clients when I moved to the private sector.

15

Show Me the Money: Asset Investigations

Throughout the book, we have discussed ways to protect yourself before you make an investment, hire an executive, loan money, or ink a deal. But what happens when the money is already on the table, and when you look to recoup your investment, you are told the money is no longer there? Or, what if you have a hunch there is more (or less) money in the pockets of the person you are about to invest in? Asset investigations empower you with the necessary information about an individual's financial structure and assist you in targeting your pursuit.

The Situation: Going for Broke

KindBank gave a real estate developer in California a $7 million loan for construction on new development properties in the southern part of the state. Jim Imbroke, the developer, promised to repay the loan in a period of five years. A few months after the loan was in default, Jim Imbroke met with his bankers at KindBank and said, "Listen, fellas, the truth is I have no money. The market has changed, my deals fell through, and I can no longer repay the money I owe you. Any chance we can strike a deal and settle the loan for five cents on the dollar?"

The associates at KindBank knew the real estate market had taken a dive. They thought about Imbroke's proposal and realized it was better for them to recoup *some* of their money than to have a complete loss. So KindBank told Imbroke it would accept his offer. A few days after striking the verbal agreement with Imbroke, Kindbank's outside counsel called us. KindBank wanted us to run a preliminary asset search just to confirm that Imbroke was as strapped for cash as he presented himself to be.

As part of our methodology, we ran property records and did not find anything of substance owned by Imbroke (although we found Imbroke did own some properties, all of these parcels of property were encumbered). Next we ran some court record searches. Court records do not reap results that *directly* relate to an individual's asset structure; however, they do provide information that can *indicate* whether an individual or company is in financial distress. Whether we find bankruptcy filings, liens, judgments, or UCC filings, these records can tell us that the person or company has been unable to make payments to others. So for Imbroke, that is exactly what we found. Imbroke had several state tax liens and civil judgments filed by subcontractors that had never been paid. This seemed to indicate that Imbroke was, indeed, unable to repay the KindBank loan.

We then decided to look at some of Imbroke's business associates from over the years. Initially, we thought these individuals would either have valuable information regarding Imbroke's asset structure or would be able to point us in the direction of someone who was privy to this type of information. Instead, we found something much better: a newly formed real estate development company in California named Poleved that was formed by a former business partner of Imbroke's. Poleved's website boasted the roster of the company's talented and experienced team, and Jim Imbroke was named as a principal of the Poleved team (even though he was not named on the company's corporate record). We started to do more research on Poleved and found that a local real estate trade publication just announced Poleved was among the final bidders on a large state government contract. Because government contracts are public record information, we were able to determine that all final bidders on this contract were required to demonstrate that the principals had a net worth in excess of $10 million. So Jim Imbroke had told KindBank he had no money, yet he had signed a government document attesting to having a net worth of more than $10 million.

We presented the information to the outside counsel of Kind-Bank and suggested we join them in meeting with Imbroke when they were scheduled to execute the original agreement of repayment of the loan for five cents on the dollar. At the meeting, the KindBank associates sat at the table with Imbroke and watched as he took out his personal checkbook and began to write the date on the check for the negotiated repayment. Before the check was signed, the attorney for KindBank leaned in to Imbroke and said, "Just wanted to let you know that we have an obligation to go to the California Building Standards Commission to tell them that you apparently falsified the document stating you have an exorbitant net worth because you're saying in our documents here that you don't have any money." Without blinking, Imbroke filled out the check for the entire amount owed to KindBank.

The Tactic: The Property Paper Trail

It is always wise for people to protect their assets. You know this. But when loans are in default and financial agreements are being ignored, the line between protecting assets and hiding assets is slim. To recoup monies owed from loans or equity investments and in the instance of recourse loans, attorneys, investment firms, and financial institutions hire us to conduct asset investigations to identify any assets owned by the person that may be of relevance. Of course, without authorization, we cannot access private banking records but, like anything else, it takes a little creativity and a lot of experience to know where to find the money.

As you saw with Jim Imbroke, property records are public record information. Every county in every state has a different system of compiling these records, but LexisNexis and Westlaw have an impressive collection of property records filed throughout the country. We always call the local tax assessor or appropriate state/county department to get the most current property information because the online records may not have been updated in a timely manner.

Finding Hidden Assets in the Real Estate Business

Corporate Resolutions has worked with banks to help identify an individual's assets when that person or entity claims he or she can no longer repay the loan. And we have found that banks may not always verify the assets or the financial stability of the borrower before the loan is made. When seeking to identify assets, sometimes the person is, indeed, without any assets, yet it is also often the case that these cries of poverty are unsubstantiated. For instance, many financial institutions provided multi-million dollar loans to real estate developers at the height of the residential market in booming cities, such as Miami. Profits seemed rather promising. Within a year, however, the landscape changed. Many projects halted midway through construction as the subprime mortgage crisis hit and fewer people were able to pay the soaring prices of apartments. Despite a developer's earnest efforts to proceed with the project, the market could no longer support all of the projects at once. Nonetheless, the banks that provided the initial loans still needed to recoup their investment. Some developers were new players in the development space and had riskily put all of their investments, both personal and professional, into the success of the project. Other experienced developers ran into cash flow problems (could not make payroll or pay subcontractors and suppliers), knew the business was in trouble long before the banks got wind of it, and began to shelter assets, knowing one day the banks would come knocking. This is where we come in.

Banks hire investigative companies to determine if a developer has any assets that would enable him or her to repay the bank loan. We have found that real estate developers generally know six to nine months in advance if they are going under and accordingly make plans to hide their assets. They often form new entities for each project to limit their liability, and they also can take equity in condos at every different project. If a developer is working on four different properties, then there will typically be at least four different companies that have been formed by the developer, and the company names often reflect the address where the development is taking place (for example, 123 Main Street, LLC). With this in mind, when we undergo our asset search we start by identifying any addresses used by the developer. This information comes to us through identifiers and business and media sources.

Local newspapers and trade magazines are great sources of information when developments are planned in a specific area because developers want to create necessary buzz for the project, so as to entice future investors and buyers/renters. For instance, *The Real Deal* focuses on real estate in New York City and provides updates of any and all scheduled projects in the area. Through these sources, we identify where the developer is active and then search corporate records to see all of the entities that were formed for each development project. For the older development projects, the corporate records show the corresponding company as inactive or delinquent. But because you are required to pay taxes on active companies, we can identify active companies that correlate to active projects owned or managed by the developer. Each company can represent a potential asset: Either the developer will earn money if/when the project is complete, or the developer can hold bank accounts in the name of these companies. This is one of the tricks when finding assets for real estate developers. Asset searches, like the situation with Jim Imbroke, do not always uncover specific assets owned by an individual but rather find information that gives you leverage in a situation.

The Situation: The Driver Has the Keys

We were once hired to run an asset search on an elderly couple who owed money to a private investor. When we searched our trove of public record sources, we did not find the couple had any assets in their individual names. The couple, however, had lived a lavish life in the 1980s and had paid off the mortgage for their large townhouse on the Upper East Side of New York City. We were able to find out that the couple had recently laid off a number of former employees, including their longtime private chauffeur. We located the driver, and when we spoke with him and asked him if he knew anything about the financial status of the couple, the driver said, "Hop in. I will show you the bank I drove them to on Mondays, the other bank I drove them to on Tuesdays, and the third and fourth banks I would drive them to at the end of the week. Oh, and I know what names each bank account is under."

The Tactic: Human Sources

Former employees have proven to us to be great troves of information. While not every lead we follow brings us to a driver with secrets ready to be unloaded, we do find former employees who know about a person's hobbies, spending habits, or travel schedules. This could mean unearthing a person's affinity for gambling or jetting to the Cayman Islands for vacation, both of which are clues as to where money is spent or kept. If they are going to the Caymans, maybe they have bank accounts or own property there and do not declare those assets on U.S. tax documents so as to avoid paying taxes. Because there is no research vehicle to find where someone banks internationally, contacting former employees or attempting to discern a person's travel habits are some of the best ways to find out or at least to develop information that points you in the right direction. You never know where the research will lead, but whether circuitous or direct, the information inevitably leads you to the right answers.

Offshore Accounts

Places like the Cayman Islands, the Channel Islands, the Isle of Man, Luxembourg, and Mauritius are common hot spots where people hide assets.

Methods for Finding Assets

Corporate records always represent potential assets for an individual, but not many people outside of the real estate world, the oil and gas industry, and the restaurant sphere have the tendency or need to form numerous companies. For these individuals, our asset searches are initially focused on property records, vehicle registration records, and other various nontraditional sources. Before we run any asset searches, we must confirm identifying information on a person to get a track record of addresses the person has used over the last 10 or 20 years. This lets us know where to start when we review property records. We always look to see if the person owns his or her current residence and, if the home is not in the name of the subject, then who owns the property.

If Harry Home lives at 789 Elm Street, we find the property record for 789 Elm Street. If we find that Harry Home does not own the house, but rather that Elm Street Properties owns the house, we then review corporate records to find out who is the owner of Elm Street Properties. The research is multitiered.

Once we find this information about Harry Home's current residence, the same steps are taken for every other address identified for Harry Home, as well as for the addresses where the taxes are sent (that is, if Harry Home's property taxes for 789 Elm Street are sent to 456 Generic Street, then we will see who owns 456 Generic Street). What we end up with is a list of properties bought and sold by Harry Home over the years.

We also look to see when properties were sold. If we find Harry Home *currently* owns no real properties, we look to see when he sold the properties he previously owned. What if he sold them all on, or around, the same date? What if he transferred the properties to be in the name of his wife, children, or company via an interfamily transfer that can be done by way of a quitclaim deed or warranty deed? These would be indicators that Harry Home is attempting to shelter his assets or be judgment proof.

In the case of Jim Imbroke, we talked about searching for judgments and liens filed against a person, which indicate that person is struggling financially. Another resource to this end is the U.S. Tax Court, which has a searchable website that allows you to see if a person has been sued by or has sued the Commissioner of Internal Revenue. While sometimes these cases are merely routine, in other instances, the cases can be indicators that someone has tried to avoid paying taxes, is attempting to devalue property assessed at a high value, or other issues that shed light on a person's asset structure and character.

Another spot we hit when looking for assets is vehicle, boat, and airplane registrations (does Harry Home drive a Ferrari? a yacht? a single-engine plane?). If we find through the Federal Aviation Administration (FAA) that Harry Home has a pilot's license, it is only logical that we search to see if he owns a private plane. Both Harry's license and his plane can be identified through the FAA website (www.faa.gov).

We also look to see if Harry Home has made political contributions. If he is claiming he has no money, then how is he able to donate to his favorite political candidate? Political contributions are easily accessed through the Federal Election Commission (www.fec.gov). There are a few websites that allow you to see if a person has made any contributions to political parties/campaigns over the years. The Federal Election Commission is the first place we go to search for these contributions. However, there are other websites that have different ways to search contributions, such as by address, by company, and so on. These websites are opensecrets.org, newsmeat.com, followthemoney.org, and campaignmoney.com.

We also determine if Harry Home has had any patents or trademarks registered in his name. These patents and trademarks are a form of intellectual property, and in many cases can be purchased (or sold) for sizable sums of money. The U.S. Patent and Trademark Office has a great website, http://www.uspto.gov/, that allows you to search for patents and trademarks, and the information tells you not only the name of the inventor(s) but also when it was filed and who the trademark or patent was assigned to (quite often this is a company).

Websites As Assets

Domain names are another form of intellectual property. You can check to see if a person or company has registered domain names. This search tells you the dates the domain names were reserved and the person(s) to which the names are registered. Among other things, identifying domain name registrations can help determine a person's intent to start a new business. These can be found by searching the WHOIS database at http://www.networksolutions.com/whois/index.jsp.

These are some of the basic research tools we use when conducting asset investigations. With asset searches, as with all of our other investigations, a single component of research is never enough. The research must be done comprehensively, the information must be analyzed repeatedly, and the sources must be accessed properly in order to reap the best results.

16

Investigating the Inc.

So far we have focused primarily on individuals who have engaged in misconduct on some level. But what if you are investing in or acquiring a company? Do you need to do a background check on the company too? Yes.

If you are investing in a company, you have probably looked at the company's balance sheet, analyzed the revenue stream, and examined other financial aspects of the company. But conducting investigative research on the company is also a critical step. Like the results from our research on management teams, the information we find about a company can also impact a deal.

Some of the issues you need to uncover include a company's involvement in active lawsuits. If a lawsuit is active at the time of your acquisition or investment, you need to know the ramifications of the case. How much time (and money) will the company need to devote to participating in the active case? Does the case involve an issue that may impact the success of the company or its reputation, such as a patent infringement (will your target company lose its rights to market a product) and securities class action cases (will this result in sizable fines or monies owed to plaintiffs)?

When we look at a company's involvement in lawsuits, we also focus on cases that have been closed. Does the company have a pattern of being sued and then settling out of court? This could affect your deal as the company would be spending lots of money on unnecessary legal fees. Or we look at the dates civil cases or judgments were closed or paid off to see if the company has deliberately tried to resolve all of its legal issues within a few months of seeking funding.

Regulatory issues are also common findings in our research. It is important for you to be aware if the company has been fined by any regulatory agencies and to confirm the certifications the company claims it has been awarded. All of these matters play a vital role in the company's future and are not always brought to your attention when you are in negotiations with the company.

The Situation: Submitting to a Scam

We have all engaged in some form of online shopping. No matter the product, you know the drill: Click on the item you want to buy, go to your "shopping cart," input your name, billing, and shipping addresses, your credit card information, review your purchase again, click "submit" (or some variation of that) and, within minutes, you receive an email confirming the details of your transaction.

What if you were unknowingly charged the second you clicked on the item? If, for example, you were looking for a book and found that *Digging for Disclosure* sounded interesting but wanted to read more about it before you made your purchase, you would click the icon for the book and get more details. If you were buying the book on ETricks, you would have just been charged for the book.

ETricks was a company we investigated, along with the members of the company's management team. ETricks' scam described here was unknown to our client, who was looking to acquire the company. We found out that the Federal Trade Commission (FTC) sued ETricks a few months prior to our client beginning negotiations with the company. The docket sheet for the federal case said it had been settled. When we ran our review of disciplinary actions filed by regulatory agencies both nationally and internationally, we found out more details.

The FTC had received complaints about ETricks, conducted its own investigation about the complaints, filed a suit against ETricks, and the matter was settled when ETricks agreed to pay a $4 million fine for engaging in the deceitful game of secretly charging its customers before they pressed the Submit button. Our client was unaware of the fines, the charges by the FTC, or the fact that the company engaged in such practices. The client decided to look for a different online opportunity.

The Tactic: Regulators Rule

We always contact regulatory agencies and other appropriate compliance departments to confirm a company has not been involved in any illicit practices. In the case of ETricks, the FTC is what helped guide our investigation. The Better Business Bureau is a quick way to check if a company has had any consumer complaints filed against it. When checking on companies that do business directly with consumers, this is a good resource.

The Occupational Safety and Health Administration (OSHA) website is also a tool we often use. OSHA ensures companies do not have hazardous workplaces or job sites and is tasked with overseeing the safety of employees. OSHA conducts routine inspections at companies and has a record of any violations a company has received, complaints filed, inspections conducted, and the results of these actions. When you look at these OSHA records, you can see if a company has

Deal S.O.S.

The information gathered on a company does not always kill a deal. Sometimes if you find the company has been involved in controversial issues, the information assists you in gaining leverage during your negotiations. In the situation of ETricks, you could have used the information about the FTC to either try and pay less for the company or insist the company change its practices, implement a Code of Ethics policy, and force the company to agree to abide by strict policies you provide.

been in violation of OSHA standards and whether the company has had to pay fines and/or has properly fixed the problem. Again, this affects your deal. If a company has had repeat problems and has been fined by OSHA, this could mean the company is recklessly spending money on OSHA fines and not fixing the problem, or it could end up that an employee is harmed on the job because of its shoddy conditions, and the employee sues, thus causing your company unnecessary negative publicity, embarrassment, and expensive legal fees.

When conducting inquiries on companies or individuals involved in the financial community, there are several fundamental regulatory resources that have easily searchable websites for you to access information. The Securities Exchange Commission (SEC) is responsible for overseeing the securities industry and related stock and options exchanges. The website, www.sec.gov, allows you to search to identify any companies that are registered as investment advisors with the SEC (which applies to many hedge funds). When a firm is registered as an investment adviser with the SEC, the Form ADVs (as they are called) are available for free to the public, online on the SEC website. When properly executed by the firm, these Form ADVs provide detailed information on the owners and indirect owners, the approximate amount of monies invested in the fund, affiliate funds, and any previous disciplinary actions taken against the owners or the fund, and often these documents list service providers to the firm/fund; that is, fund administrators, prime brokers, accountants, attorneys, and so on.

To determine if an individual or company is licensed as a broker, you can search the website of the Financial Industry Regulatory Authority (FINRA), formerly known as the National Association of Securities Dealers (NASD). FINRA is an independent regulatory body that oversees financial brokers and securities firms and has its own searchable website. The FINRA website allows you to search for an individual or firm to identify registrations, violations, arbitrations, and a host of additional free information available on the company or person.

Just as the SEC and FINRA are involved in overseeing the financial services industry, there are numerous state and federal regulatory agencies that are responsible for ensuring companies are in compliance with state and federal laws in almost every industry. For companies involved in banking, we check with appropriate state and federal banking departments, and similarly when checking out companies involved in the insurance industry, we contact appropriate state insurance departments to find out what is on record for the company. When we are conducting inquiries on companies that are in the food services or pharmaceutical industries, we reach out to the Food and Drug Administration (FDA) to see what is available with the FDA about the company. If we are looking into a company that has a product that affects the environment (dry cleaning companies, waste or recycling companies), we reach out to the Environmental Protection Agency (EPA) and determine if the EPA has any information about the subject company. And if we are checking out a company in communications (broadcast, radio, Internet, and so on), we contact the Federal Communications Commission (FCC) to identify any complaints filed against the company and to confirm licenses issued by the FCC.

A list of regulatory agencies we frequently use is provided in the Resource Guide, but some of these other agencies include the following:

- **General Services Administration (GSA).** When companies are involved in working for the government, the GSA maintains a database of companies that have been excluded from working for the government. The website, https://www. epls.gov/, allows you to search to see if any companies have been barred from working for the federal government.

- **Office of Foreign Assets Control (OFAC).** This is a department of the U.S. Treasury and is responsible for ensuring companies and individuals who work in foreign countries are in compliance with U.S. regulations. OFAC often works with foreign governments and is responsible for administering sanctions against the companies or individuals who are in

violation of U.S. policies. Through its website, http://www.
ustreas.gov/offices/enforcement/ofac/, OFAC maintains records of all sanctions it has handed down.

- **United States Patent and Trademark Office.**   This agency
keeps track of every patent and trademark filed in the United
States. Companies (and individuals) frequently rely on their
respective patents and trademarks as the cornerstone of business. In asset searches, we always search for patents and trademarks, as this is a form of intellectual property and has value.
The department has a website, http://www.uspto.gov/, that is easily searchable and allows you to identify or confirm any patents
or trademarks assigned to companies or individuals (as discussed
in Chapter 15, "Show Me the Money: Asset Investigations).

These are just some of the regulatory bodies that we regularly
contact to learn more about a company and to make sure the subject
company is in compliance and not subject to anything that would negatively affect its ability to perform.

In previous chapters, we have discussed our search strategies and
how we find former employees of a company who have given great
insight into the operations of a company. These former employees are
identified when we conduct research on the company. And as we
have pointed out, former employees often have internal information
about a company that would not otherwise be known.

We were looking into a company that was about to be acquired
and found out it was ensnared in an ugly political mess because of the
actions of the former CEO. The CEO had left two years before our
client was looking to invest, but the issue only recently came up
because of an investigation into one of these political figures. None of
the *current* officers were involved, so had we just focused our investigation on the current management team, we would not have uncovered the problem.

There are many resources we use to make sure the company with
which you are about to do business will perform accordingly. Overlooking a background check on the company can mean overlooking
critical information that might impact your deal.

17 ————————————————————

You, the Referee

At Corporate Resolutions, we do not think the information relayed in the background check process is the only thing that drives a deal. You are familiar with the financial aspects of the deal, the legal intricacies, and other liabilities that come into play. Sometimes we may think the information we gather will kill or rescue a deal, but we often only know a small percentage of what is going on in the locker room of the business agreement.

We have been involved in deals where we have uncovered a CEO who was arrested for grand theft, or a COO who had spent years struggling with an addiction to heroin, but the deal still goes through. Conversely, we have seen clients cancel a deal when an executive had two Driving Under the Influence charges, or a fund manager who had several outstanding tax liens. These decisions are based on your own personal judgment, your inner moral compass and, sometimes, just maybe your hunch—and we may not always agree with you.

The Situation: Fraud vs. Brothel: You Choose

At the beginning of 2009, when the markets were shaky and deal flow was pretty dry, an investment adviser was looking to invest in a hedge fund run by Clark Chance, an East Coast native who was pretty well established in the investment world. The investor had friends who had invested in Clark Chance and had seen sizable returns on their investment. Our client wanted in, but before he committed to Clark Chance, he asked us to run a background check.

We did not find any regulatory actions, civil cases, criminal matters, or bankruptcy filings for Chance, or even any companies he had not already disclosed to our client. We found many media articles that lauded Chance for his brilliant investments over the years. In the midst of the media articles, we found an article from the late 1980s with the headline: "Group of Bankers Arrested at Local Brothel." According to the article, Clark Chance was "entertaining" a client by taking him to a brothel—on the same day that the brothel was raided by the local police. Everyone at the brothel was arrested. The incident was not found in our criminal record searches because we searched criminal records in the areas where Chance had lived and worked within the last ten years. The brothel was located in a completely different state and because we had not found Chance in that state, we had no reason to run criminal record searches there. Nonetheless, we quickly called the local courthouse and the local police and requested copies of any and all information about the matter from their archives. While we waited for the documents to arrive, we met with our client.

As we told our client, our issue was not only that Chance went to the brothel but that he had the poor judgment to bring the client. The investor disagreed. As someone familiar with the "entertaining" practices of some people in the financial community, the investor did not think Chance's behavior was so outlandish. The investor asked us to continue with our investigation and let him know when the archived documents from the case came in.

A week later, the documents arrived, and we read more about what took place that day. The story in the arrest report was not much different from what was relayed in the media article we found. Again, the brothel incident occurred in a different state than where Chance resided. But because the incident happened almost 15 years prior and our criminal record searches typically go back seven to ten years, we decided we needed to err on the side of caution and expand the scope of our initial criminal record searches. So we reran all of our criminal record searches and searched the archived criminal records to see if Chance had been involved in any matters that were filed more than ten years ago. And, in fact, he had been.

We received a copy of an arrest report from a local police station, and according to the officer involved and the documents we reviewed, this is what went down:

Clark Chance owned two vintage cars: a green 1965 Porsche coupe and a white 1971 Mercedes-Benz convertible. He had insurance policies on both cars that reflected the high value of these automobiles. At midnight in 1987, two years before the brothel incident, Clark Chance called the police in a panic: The vintage cars were stolen! The police came to his house and took Chance's statement, in which he said the cars were locked in his garage and someone must have broken in and taken the vehicles. Four weeks after the cars were reported stolen, a police officer was doing a routine drive-by in Chance's neighborhood and noticed Chance's garage door was left slightly open, and it seemed no one was home. Aware of the report of the stolen cars, the officer pulled over and approached Chance's garage to make sure someone had not broken in again. The officer went up to the garage and saw the *same* two vintage cars that were reported stolen. Chance had moved the cars and reported them stolen so he could cash in on his insurance policy. Subsequently, Chance was arrested and charged with insurance fraud and obstruction of justice.

When we told our client the story, he was appalled. The brothel incident he would have overlooked, but insurance fraud was something the client found to be unacceptable. Our client did not invest in Clark Chance.

This is an example of how every client's personal assessment of a situation dictates how an investment decision is made. Some investors might have blinders on and would have disregarded both incidents and invested with Chance because of the high returns

Chance promised. Other people would have walked when they found out about the brothel. Like politics and religion, everyone has a concrete sense of how he sees the world and what is, in his eyes, "right" and "wrong." These factors always come into play when doing business.

The Situation: Sex, Documents, and a Deal

We had another case where we found the subject was arrested for "disorderly conduct." When we looked at the court documents, we found the person was originally arrested for soliciting prostitution, but the charges were knocked down to "disorderly conduct." (Yes, this is the prostitution chapter.)

The documents said that the person had agreed to go to a sex addiction rehabilitation clinic and was ordered by the court to stay 200 feet away from a specific corner in the city where he was arrested. Because of the sentence the person received, it was clear that this was not his first time soliciting prostitution. Did the client do the deal? Yep. The client felt that the incident did not impact the person's ability to perform and had faith the person had undergone rehab and deserved a second chance.

The Situation: Thieves Then; Executives Now

A private equity (PE) firm was looking to acquire a hardware company in Oregon. The PE firm asked us to check out the two brothers who founded the company: Steve and Dave Abind. The company, Abind Brothers, was small, and there was very little information available about the company. Steve and Dave Abind had spent their entire lives in the same modest town in Oregon where they were born. Their father originally started the company, and when he passed away, Steve and Dave Abind took over and started to expand the roster of items sold at the store. Steve and Dave were both married, and they each had young kids. They had both started working for Abind Brothers when they were young, and they had never worked for any other companies. While all of this seemed like a fine and simple story, the perspective changed when we learned that Steve had been arrested for stealing a pick-up truck when he was 23 years old, and Dave had been arrested for armed robbery when he was 28 years old. Both Steve and Dave had served time in a state penitentiary for their respective crimes. When we told the client about the trouble the Abind brothers had been in, the client said, "But they weren't involved in drugs, right?"

Right. Steve and Dave Abind were not involved in drugs. The client rationalized that the brothers grew up in the type of neighborhood/family/environment where theft and robbery were not outrageous indicators of bad business acumen or an inability to run a hardware company. The client went ahead with their acquisition, and the Abinds and our client still retain a harmonious business relationship.

The Tactic: Assessing Your Appetite

Yes, we have discussed media articles before. But in the instance of Clark Chance we see how media articles navigated us to a criminal background that would not have been uncovered if we had relied solely on court record searches. It was the synthesis of conducting archived media searches, court record reviews, and contacting local authorities that led us to the actual story about Clark Chance's past. When criminal records have been expunged, it is often media sources and interviews with industry and law enforcement sources that lead us to the existence of these cases.

We mentioned the case of the person who was originally charged with soliciting prostitution but the charges were knocked down to disorderly conduct. The information available in the court indices only provided the charges to which the person pled guilty. It was only when we requested to review the documents on file in the criminal case that we learned about the prostitution charges.

With the Abinds, we understood the client's willingness to forgive these criminal histories and move forward with the deal. There are always extraneous circumstances that must be taken into account when making business decisions. There have been times, however, when we have repeatedly cautioned a client to reconsider the deal based on information we found. In one instance we found that a money manager had served time in federal prison for stealing money from investors, and our client did not think the information was pertinent to his deal. But the operative word is *his* deal. He knew the money manager's background and said he intended to structure the deal to place certain limits on him. The client was willing to take that risk. Again, it all comes down to your comfort level.

It used to be that companies would hire us to conduct discreet background checks without the subject's knowledge of our investigative research. Within the last few years however, between the requirements of Sarbanes-Oxley and Know Your Customer and the increases in corporate fiduciary responsibilities, most of our clients now tell the individuals up front that a background check will be conducted on them before the deal. This allows the investor to show that he/she is serious about the investment, and allows the candidate to be up front with any issues that may have happened in the past. It is now viewed as practical and wise for investors to conduct background checks, bringing them to the foreground.

In any transaction in which you are looking to become involved, you are the one to make the final call. Everyone has a different appetite for risk. We have worked with clients who deal primarily in distressed investments, or "vulture funds," and they are aware that problems exist at the company; for them, the higher the risk, the better. No matter what type of investment you are making, however, the information that unfolds in a background check helps you know everything before moving forward. Sometimes if we do uncover negative information, this can help you restructure the terms of the deal, implement appropriate checks and balances, or simply understand what additional contingencies need to be considered. You should always investigate before you invest. The best advice we can give you is awareness: Be aware of the situation and consider all of the information you have. As they say, "Better the devil you know, than the devil you don't."

18

The Secret Sauce

We have discussed instances of varying degrees of fraud that we have uncovered during our many years of conducting business investigations and also touched on some recent well known business scams. We have told you what happened, how it happened, and what could have been avoided from our professional perspective. But how do we do it? What do we look for? What is the recipe for our secret investigative sauce, and how can you apply our methods to your own due diligence initiatives?

No matter the nature of our inquiry, we always rely on two unique approaches to gathering intelligence and determining what needs to be done to give a client their required comfort level: our creative research strategies and our analysis of information. There are thousands of public record sources available to anyone at any time. Google is an easy and popular resource where you can throw an individual's name or a company name into the search bar and probably find out something you did not already know. For those of you who have access to commercial databases such as LexisNexis or Bloomberg terminals, you know that these resources provide an enormous amount of information. But what you have access to is just as significant as how you use it.

Take the story of Howard Deepart (from Chapter 3, "We Call That a Clue"), the CFO who defrauded a company of millions of dollars by siphoning funds from his legitimate employer to another company with a similar name that he had formed. The corporate record for this other company, the vehicle Deepart used to perpetrate his

fraud, did not list Deepart's name on the document. Instead, the corporate record just listed Deepart's home address. Had we just used
Deepart's name as our search strategy, we never would have uncovered the key to the fraud. As in all of our searches, we use the individual's name as a starting point. Once we establish where a person has
lived and worked for the past ten years or so, we also use those
addresses as search terms. Deepart needed to form a company in
order to open a bank account for his stolen funds. Corporate records
are filed by the state and are available for public review. In most
states, the Secretary of State oversees the formation of companies.
Many states have websites that allow you to access and search their
databases of corporate documents. LexisNexis also has a comprehensive collection of Secretary of State records filed in 48 states.

However, as previously stated, there are two states that do not
have corporate records accessible through LexisNexis and must be
accessed through the respective state websites: New Jersey and
Delaware. Delaware is a very common place for companies to be
formed (more than half of the Fortune 500 companies are incorpo-
rated in Delaware). The state of Delaware has certain tax rules and
other laws that are favorable for companies (some people refer to
Delaware as a "tax haven" for corporations). Further, Delaware does
not require a company to list officers or directors on corporate
records. Because these records are not available through LexisNexis,
they must be accessed separately via the website at http://corp.
delaware.gov. It provides you the opportunity to purchase status and
tax reports and historical information on the company. Also, given
that most New Jersey corporate records are not included in
LexisNexis, if we find an individual has lived or worked in New Jersey, we conduct a separate search with the New Jersey Secretary of
State to identify any entities filed in New Jersey that list the individual as an officer, director, or registered agent. These records are
accessed through the New Jersey website at https://accessnet.state.nj.
us/home.asp.

Because of our intimate familiarity with corporate wrongdoing, we know what to look for: Avoiding using personal names on legal documents, such as corporate records, is just one way that scammers try to succeed. To thoroughly protect our clients and give them the necessary information, we apply our sophisticated search strategies to all available public records, such as searching corporate records by addresses and not just names.

To quote *The Sound of Music*: "Let's start at the very beginning, a very good place to start." For us, the beginning of any investigation starts with running what we call "identifiers" (we have mentioned identifiers in previous chapters). These are databases that identify and confirm a person's name, date of birth, recent addresses, and a fragment of the person's Social Security number. Not only do these identifiers assist us when specifically tasked with locating people, but also they play an indispensable role in setting the stage of the investigation. Arrowgant, Speed, Freenclear, Sneaks, Deepart, Leader, Omit, Front, Grudge, Guile, Legitt, Axtagrinde, Surprise, Bucks, Wicked, Hoax, Chance, Abind, Fikshun, Shady, and Imbroke: In every one of these stories, our investigative performance relied on the first step we took. Had we mistakenly begun our investigations on someone else who had the same name as any of these characters, our clients would have deemed us inadequate, not to mention we could have wrongfully accused many people of misconduct.

So what are these "identifiers," and how do they work? The sources we use compile legally available information from credit-reporting and other sources and provide a profile of a person. If you put Penelope Bucks in the search, you will find every person with the name "Penelope Bucks" across the country. Once you choose which Penelope Bucks is the person you are investigating (based on known address history and age), you can look at more information on *that* Penelope Bucks. The profile for Bucks will show you all of the addresses Bucks has used in the last ten or so years, and a few other tidbits of available information. As licensed private investigators, we

have access to certain information that is not available to most companies. And as responsible investigators, we are sensitive to the constant
threats of identity theft and use the information we find cautiously.
(For those of you concerned with privacy, do not worry, the information is not mainstream and is always and only used when we are conducting professional investigations.)

We use multiple identifier databases and always make sure the
information we have from one source mirrors information from other
sources. This guarantees the accuracy of our reports. When we have a
signed release from a subject (which allows us to review consumer
credit reports), we ask the individual to provide his or her Social
Security number, date of birth, and current address. Then when we
review our identifier sources, we can make sure the information
matches. Sometimes, believe it or not, people have lied about their
dates of birth or Social Security numbers. When this happens, it is an
immediate red flag. If John Jokers tells us his Social Security number
is 123-45-6789 and we find it is really 123-45-6788 (one digit off), we
will run *both* numbers in all of our searches to see what comes up for
the other number. In other instances, we have found the name a person supplied does not match the Social Security number. We once did
an investigation on John, only to find out when we were confirming
education that John did not receive a degree from the school, but *Jill*
did. Because the school kept their records by Social Security number
and not just by names, we found out that John was once Jill. How
funny is this one?

The information we get from identifiers gives us a jumping point:
The address history tells us where to search courts and criminal
records, as each address is used to find property ownership, corporate interests, and so on. This information is only useful when it is
cross-referenced and properly interpreted. Consistent with all of our
search strategies, identifying information on a subject must be analyzed and not merely read.

Another way our search strategies and analysis come into play is when we conduct media searches. We access four different major news databases (LexisNexis, Bloomberg, Factiva, and Westlaw), which allows us to review articles published in thousands of local, national, and international newspapers, magazines, journals, trade publications, transcripts from television news programs, and Congressional testimonies. We often find news reports that quote the individual as an employee of companies where he or she has worked over the years. This complements the employment verification process. Media articles also discuss charitable and social events in local communities, rosters of participants in sports events, and frequently mention people who have attended or hosted these events. These reports can also provide key information on a person. If Jim Smith ran a marathon or hosted a charity for impoverished children, this helps you paint a more complete picture of Jim Smith.

When we run our media searches, we look to not only identify articles that mention the subject, but also articles that mention individuals who have worked with the subject over the years. As mentioned in previous chapters, talking to former colleagues over and above a person's friendly references often provides significant information regarding the subject. If we know that Jim Smith worked in a specific department of Merrill Lynch from 1999 to 2001, then we will look to find articles that mention other people who worked in that same department at the same time as Jim Smith. Then, if the client wants to contact references for Jim Smith above and beyond the names Jim Smith provided, the co-workers we identified can be great sources of information. Also, news sources often mention an individual's corporate interests, which complements what we find through our review of corporate records and business databases. For instance, an article will mention Jim Smith is an investor in a company, or served on the board, or that many years ago Jim Smith worked as an intern at a commercial bank. If Jim Smith was an investor in a private company, then his name may not show up on that company's corporate record. Similarly, interns and other employees who are not management-level at a company will not be listed on that company's corporate records. Wedding announcements, property transfers, and other local listings also contribute to understanding a person's background. Media searches help connect a person to other companies, properties, and personal and professional relationships over the years.

As with Nicholas Cosmo (from Chapter 7, "Digging for Disclosure"), media articles also identify controversial issues that a person has been involved in. Even when the topic is not as mainstream as Cosmo's connections, articles from small local newspapers play a crucial role in identifying an individual's involvement in disreputable activity. These local papers and other regional media databases have police blotters that often highlight when someone has been arrested or charged with criminal behavior, as we saw with Clark Chance (Chapter 17, "You, the Referee"). These cases may not come up when we run our court record searches because the charges may have been dropped and the case never went to court, or may have been filed more than 15 years ago (when court records often are put into archives and/or are not readily available in our classic 10-year court record reviews). We have found people who are now in their mid-40s who were arrested for DUI or assault when they were in college. And this information was uncovered through local media sources, not initially through the court or criminal system. Also as discussed in Chapter 15, "Show Me the Money: Asset Investigations," when conducting asset searches, trade publications can play an integral role, especially when we are looking at real estate developers.

If we have not already made our point about the omnipotent media sources, consider the genealogy of these publications. If you rely on Google searches or other Internet sources, you are probably only going to get select media articles published within the last ten years or so. But when you use commercial databases like the ones described here, you find articles published from the early 1900s to the present. These publications have transferred their microfiche archives and sold them to companies such as LexisNexis, and thus provide us with a trove of media sources. We learned about Clark Chance's criminal background because of the older media articles we uncovered. When looking into someone's background, you do not want a time limit on the information. An individual's background does not expire, and neither should your sources of information.

As discussed in Chapter 3, confirming an individual's accomplishments, such as education and professional licenses, is critical. As enumerated in that chapter, people will fudge their credentials more often than you think. There is one main clearinghouse used by colleges and universities for education verification: National Student Clearinghouse. This company has an easy-to-use website, www. studentclearinghouse.org, that allows you to confirm most degrees received by an individual and gives you enrollment information. Some schools still require signed releases from the individual in order to confirm a degree, but the National Student Clearinghouse gives you clear instructions on which schools require what type of information. Some schools still perform verifications in-house, in which case we independently contact the registrar for enrollment and degree information. When we find inconsistencies with information presented on a resume and information provided by a school, we always request authorized documentation from the school to confirm what was relayed to us to avoid any errors or false accusations of resume fraud.

To confirm someone is a licensed Certified Public Accountant (CPA), Chartered Financial Analyst (CFA), or other designation, there are specific state or institutional websites that provide contact information to confirm these licenses. For instance, if someone claims he or she is a licensed CPA in New York, we would call or search the website of the New York State Education Department, Office of the Professions.

In Chapter 7, we also discussed the case of Thomas Fikshun and how he lied about serving in the United States Navy. Unfortunately, this happens quite often. We have seen many instances where individuals have falsely claimed service in the U.S. military. To avoid being fooled, you should always confirm a person has in fact served and was honorably discharged. To do so, you can submit a request with the National Archives and Records Administration.

In Chapter 16, "Investigating the Inc.," we talk about the availability of information through state and federal regulatory agencies. Specifically, we mention regulatory information available with the Financial Industry Regulatory Authority (FINRA) and the investment adviser forms on file with the Securities Exchange Commission (SEC). This information can be accessed through the respective websites for FINRA and the SEC: www.finra.org and ww.sec.gov. Many other regulatory agencies have websites that provide information on individuals in the financial community, such as the National Futures Association (NFA). This website, www.nfa.futures.org, offers a check for registrations of firms or individuals conducting futures-related business. The check includes disciplinary history from both the NFA and the Commodities Futures Trading Commission (CFTC). The Chicago Board Options Exchange (CBOE) also maintains a history of disciplinary actions taken by the CBOE against registered member firms and brokers. Similarly, when we are conducting inquiries in the United Kingdom, we rely on the Financial Services Authority (FSA) to obtain information on individuals in the financial industry.

We have also discussed the importance of searching court and criminal records on the state and federal levels in jurisdictions where a person has lived and worked over a ten-year period. We detailed how to access court records on the federal level through PACER in Chapter 7. On the state level, some states, such as Florida, Connecticut, Colorado, and Virginia, provide easy access to records through online databases available to the public. Other states, such as New York and Pennsylvania, offer a statewide criminal search that can be searched online.

We *never* rely on websites that offer "nationwide searches" of court or criminal records; these sites are not comprehensive. In certain states, the records available online only include matters that have been closed (and thus do not include any active cases); in other states, often the online court and criminal record database does not include matters filed more than three years ago. No matter where we are conducting our court and criminal record searches, we always complement our online searching with dispatching local court record retrievers to physically walk into the respective courthouse or civil record repository and search the indices to ensure efficacy and accuracy of the information.

As in the case of Sam and Mike Surprise, we found that Mike Surprise had served time in a federal prison. We did this by searching criminal records not only where he currently lived but also where he lived and worked years ago. And to determine if and when Surprise had been in a federal prison, like Andrew Shady, we accessed the inmate locator system that allowed us to search for an individual and find out the details of the sentence and the release date. As mentioned in Chapter 5, "Sometimes You Just Gotta Ask," this is a great complement to PACER when you think someone served time in prison a long time ago. We have also discussed the sex offender registries. These registries are easily searchable in most states and alert you to any known sex offenders in a specific area.

When talking about criminal records, you cannot ignore the myth of an "expunged" record. On November 11, 2009, *The Wall Street Journal* reported that more states are receiving requests by individuals and/or their attorneys to expunge their criminal records. But when a record is expunged, that does not necessarily mean the record does not exist in the public domain. When we conduct criminal record searches, whether we do them online or in person, we often uncover the arrest report or the original criminal record, and the indices may or may not have the notation that the record has been expunged. In these cases, while we might not be able to retrieve the court documents to learn more about what happened in an expunged criminal case, we do know the record exists.

In fact, and quite comically, sometimes even potential employees of our firm have not realized this. We once hired a young man, let's call him Rod Iculous, who had just graduated college. After two rounds of interviews, a writing test, and a research aptitude test, we decided to hire him on the condition that the background check came back clear. We explained this to Rod Iculous.

"Is there anything in your background that we should know about? If so, now is the time to tell us," we said.

"No," he said.

"You have never been convicted of a crime?" we asked.

"Nope," said the candidate.

So Rod Iculous signed a release form, and we told him to come back the next day to start his training and that we would simultaneously run a background check on him. At the end of the next day, the results of the criminal record search came back, showing that Rod Iculous had been arrested and convicted of drunk driving and smoking marijuana.

When we confronted him, he said, "I was told the record was expunged!" We then explained to him that Corporate Resolutions was clearly not the right spot for him, and when he said, with umbrage, "You cannot fire me because of my criminal record!"

We replied, "No, but we can fire you because you lied."

It was pretty entertaining that someone looking for a job at an investigative firm would lie about his background, knowing we would run a criminal record search. That was not the kind of employee that would fit in with the other bright analysts, and he was not the kind of employee that would properly and professionally represent us to our clients.

In Chapter 11, "Now That Is Criminal," we told the story of Penelope Bucks, who confessed she stole $100,000 from her employer, yet by the end of our investigation, we determined she in fact stole one million dollars. In that story, our review of Penelope Bucks' credit report was decisive in our analysis of Ms. Bucks' current financial situation. If you recall, Penelope Bucks said she could not pay the money back to her employer because she had gambled away the money she embezzled. When we reviewed her credit report, we saw three inquiries by casinos in Atlantic City. This confirmed, in part, Penelope Bucks' explanation of how she spent some of the money. (We have also conducted more in-depth inquiries with casinos to learn about a person's cash advances, lines of credit, and so on when an individual allows us access to this information via a signed release that authorizes us to contact casinos to retrieve this information.)

To look at someone's consumer credit report, the Fair Credit Reporting Act (FCRA) requires that the individual sign a release form allowing a third party to access his or her credit report. The FCRA is enforced by the Federal Trade Commission and is designed to ensure an individual's privacy and to protect him from identity theft. There are a few major credit reporting agencies that compile credit reports: TransUnion, ChoicePoint (now a division of LexisNexis), Experian, and Equifax. The credit reports basically look the same.

When we examine an individual's credit report, we look to see what installment and revolving accounts they maintain, what the balances are, and if they were any late payments or profit/loss write-offs. Basically, these items tell you a person's ability to pay bills and pay them on time. We examine mortgages, refinancing, and home equity loans as well as credit card accounts. If someone has had a state or federal tax lien filed against him/her, then that lien will often show up on the credit report. There have been times when we have found a lien on someone's credit report but not in our court record research (and vice versa). This has been when we have looked for court records in only one jurisdiction (at the request of a client) and the lien was filed in a different jurisdiction.

Last, as recounted earlier, we look to see who else has been looking at the person's credit report. Anytime a company looks at someone's credit report, the report shows the date of that "inquiry" (as it is called) and the company that reviewed the report. So, if you are going to lease a BMW and BMW runs a credit report on you on March 6, 2003, then we will see that on your credit report. These inquiries are important to assess because you can see if someone has a gambling line of credit (as in the case of Penelope Bucks), if there have been problems with collection companies, or if someone has applied for financing for vehicles or homes. We have also seen instances where other background check companies have made inquiries into a person's credit report.

When we are looking at multiple individuals at once, say three C-suite executives of a company, we take a look at the dates of the inquiries of each person's consumer credit report to determine if any inquiries were made on the same date for all three people. If Bank of America made an inquiry into the credit report of Kyle Hope, Matthew Gain, and Sandy Goal on November 17, 2007, we know that perhaps these three were looking to get a loan from Bank of America. And what if Bank of America decided *not* to give them a loan? Wouldn't you, as an investor or potential employer of Hope, Gain, and Goal, want to know why the bank denied their requests? In all of our reports, we bring these issues to clients' attention.

The FCRA also has strict rules when conducting background checks for pre-employment purposes. In these pre-employment background checks, information that was filed or occurred more than seven years ago is not permissible in the background check. So, if you are about to hire Kathryn Hype, a reputable accountant, and hire us to do a background check on her, we would first require Ms. Hype to sign a release form allowing us to review her consumer credit report. Then if we found in our research that Ms. Hype filed for personal bankruptcy protection 15 years ago, we would *not* be legally allowed to include that information in our report. But as with all legislation, there is fine print, and there are qualifiers to these rules. The requirements are detailed and complicated, but you can access the FCRA rules to ensure you are in compliance on the Federal Trade Commission website.

In Chapter 15 we talk about asset investigations. We use Harry Home to illustrate the ways to search property records and to identify private planes, vehicles, boats, and political contributions. Information available on property records varies by state. Some states provide details on the seller and buyer of a property, as well as the different mortgages taken on a property. These property records are available through LexisNexis and Westlaw (as well as other sources that vary by state), but in most instances, we call the local tax assessor to get the most accurate information on a home.

If Harry Home lives on 567 Front Street and the property record says he bought his house for $400,000 six years ago, we call the local tax assessor to confirm the information available online is still accurate. Also, if there are multiple parcels of land that appear related to the same property owned by Harry Home, we call the tax assessor to gain clarity on the size of the property and how the parcels are divided. Like anything else online, there may be a lag time between when the records have been updated and when the transaction occurs. This is a very common method used in mortgage fraud: Individuals will buy and sell the same property many times on the same day so as to avoid being monitored by the local tax assessor and authorities.

We have often seen that Harry Home no longer owns 567 Front Street, but The Harry Home Living Trust owns it. Property records also detail parcel numbers of properties owned. If Harry Home lives in a rural area, he probably owns his home, in addition to several acres of land that do not have a street address but are only identified through parcel numbers.

It can be overwhelmingly tiring to keep track of numerous parcel numbers and the owners of these properties, but it is always important to try and get as much information as you can from either the record itself or the tax assessor. And as we have mentioned repeatedly throughout the book, these searches cannot be performed in a vacuum. If we find Harry Home owns his residence at 567 Front Street in Los Angeles, California, and then we find The Harry Home Living Trust owns property in Las Vegas, Nevada, we then go back to our court and criminal record research and make sure we cover courts in Las Vegas. Our search strategies are constantly being amended based on what we find in each of our investigative endeavors.

These are just some of the resources and methodology we use when conducting our investigative research. But thorough research is just one piece of the puzzle. Connecting the dots and conducting analysis of information is what truly separates an investigation from a raw data dump. All of the cases mentioned in this book relied on analyses to reach the appropriate conclusions. If it were not for the rigorous dissection of data, Deepart, Sneaks, Arrowgant, and Omit would have each been just another Tom, Dick, Harry, or John.

19

Testing, Testing

Bernie Madoff. Robert Allen Stanford. Danny Pang. From the fall of 2008 through the winter of 2009, it seemed every month another scandal was uncovered that profiled how well known businessmen had victimized their clients, leaving them with nothing but a television screen to watch the scam and their bank accounts unravel. While investors were shocked, they began scratching their heads wondering how this unprecedented level of graft had come to be. Were there any warning signs? Could these massive schemes have been avoided?

Using the methodology we have discussed throughout the book, we conducted investigative research regarding Madoff, Stanford, and Pang to see if we would have come up with any red flags had we done background checks on these individuals for our clients. In each of these scams, the ringleaders went to great lengths to hide their criminal activities for their own personal greed and gain. Yet when taking a closer look at these individuals, there were a few warning signs that could have been heeded to avoid being involved in these financial disasters. As you will see, when properly executed, the investigative tools outlined in this book will help you pre-empt fraud.

The Brazen Bernie

Let's discuss the biggest: Bernie Madoff. We all know Bernie pled guilty to a Ponzi scheme that went on for over a decade and robbed investors of billions of dollars. From his closest friends and advisors to the arm's-length-friend-of-a-friend investor, Bernie successfully portrayed the persona of a reputable genius whose ability to make profits for investors was unparalleled. While some criminals rely on their salesman-like personality traits to rope unknowing victims into their lairs, Bernie relied on his aloof sensibility to perpetrate the aura that his skills were unique and any investor was truly blessed to be a part of his investors' club. The persona Bernie created for himself forced new investors to feel an element of social pressure: Who are *you* to question Bernie's tactics? Look at everyone else who has invested with him.

When conducting our research on Bernie and his related entities, we found that his lack of transparency was one of the biggest red flags we found for him. Neither investors nor regulators had access to Bernie. While we now know that he had lied for years to the Securities and Exchange Commission (SEC), Bernie's Form ADV (the form submitted to the SEC to be registered as an investment adviser) is rather lackluster. In the document, submitted on behalf of his firm, Bernard L. Madoff Investment Securities, there is scant information on Bernie himself (almost all of the required questions were left blank), no mention at all as to who was executing the trades for the firm (the fact that we now know these trades were nonexistent may explain it a little), and the only other individual listed on the form as retaining a 25% or less interest in the company is Peter Madoff, Bernie's brother. The only relevant information on this Form ADV are the two disclosure events that detail how Bernard L. Madoff Investment Securities was censured and fined $8,500 in 2007 by the National Association of Securities Dealers (NASD), now the Financial Industry Regulatory Authority (FINRA), for violating "limit order" displays, and in 2005 was censured and fined $7,000 by the NASD for failing to display customer "limit orders" that failed to comply with NASD regulations.

Beyond the void Form ADV for Bernie's firm, other red flags for Bernie Madoff include the size of the minor-league accounting firm Madoff used: a three-man operation in New City, New York (in a strip mall approximately 30 miles outside of New York City) that hardly seemed capable of overseeing billions of dollars. Further, we found that Bernie had some potential conflicts of interest with affiliate companies, such as Cohmad Securities. Cohmad Securities was supposed to have been the independent securities broker used by Bernie's firm, yet we found through our review of corporate records that both Bernie and his brother, Peter, were officers of Cohmad, and the company was located in the same suite in New York City's Lipstick Building (at 53rd Street and Third Avenue) as Madoff's investment company. While this connection was not included on the Form ADV for Bernie's firm, it was disclosed on his personal registration with FINRA (the largest independent securities regulator in the U.S.). At the least, the regulators should have asked him about his relationship to Cohmad. While there are many successful family businesses throughout the country, the fact that Bernie's brother, his sons, and his niece were among the only senior officers of the company would have given investors reason to question why the books were not opened to people outside of his family.

We also found there were numerous employees who had left Bernie's firm over the years. These former employees would have been great resources for investors and may have been exposed to some element of Bernie's scam that caused them to leave, and/or Bernie may have fired them if they had gotten too close to what was really going on.

Lastly, we found some controversial news stories reported in 2001 in *Barron's* and *MARHedge* that questioned Bernie's investment strategies. These are some of the yellow flags that would have given reason to pause before committing to Madoff. While nothing is overtly criminal, the subtleties speak volumes.

Stanford's Instabilities

Next up: Robert Allen Stanford. In February 2009, the SEC charged Robert Allen Stanford and three of his related companies with engaging in an $8 billion fraud. In essence, the SEC alleged Robert Allen Stanford, or "Sir Allen" as he preferred to be called after he was knighted in Antigua, falsely promised investors high returns on certificates of deposit. Sir Allen, a Texan native and a resident of St. Croix and Antigua, and his main company, Stanford Group Company, were well known for making sizable donations to politicians on both sides of the aisle. These politicians were also conveniently involved in international offshore banking. Stanford was also known for having a seemingly cozy relationship with regulators, specifically those in Antigua, where Sir Allen prospered.

Like Bernie Madoff, Sir Allen relied on his name and reputation to woo other investors into his fraudulent web. But what would an earnest investor have found if a little homework had been done before agreeing to hand over cash to Sir Allen?

We confirmed Stanford Group Company, an affiliate of Mr. Stanford, was registered with FINRA, and this registration (which can be accessed for free on the FINRA website) detailed numerous arbitration matters filed against Stanford Group. Specifically, between 2001 and 2006, there were seven arbitration matters in which Stanford was charged with varying degrees of fraud, including breach of fiduciary duties, negligence, omission of facts, churning, unauthorized trading, and misrepresentation. Stanford lost four of the seven arbitrations.

As if that were not enough of a reason for any investor to question Stanford, the FINRA registration also listed several actions taken by FINRA against the company. These regulatory disclosures included the following

- In 2007, the Group was censured and fined $10,000 for misrepresenting facts surrounding CD disclosures.

- In 2007, the firm's retail brokerage operation was censured and fined $20,000 for failing to meet net capital requirements and maintain adequate compliance systems, among other charges.

- In 2008, the Group was censured and fined $30,000 for multiple failures to disclose valuation methods and risks that may impede investors' ability to reach target prices as advertised.

- In 2008, the Group was censured and fined $10,000 for failing to properly report and supervise customer transactions in municipal securities.

To recap: Any investor could have hopped on the FINRA website and found that Stanford was accused of fraud on several occasions and fined by FINRA four times in less than two years for either misrepresenting facts to customers or failing to disclose proper information and strategies. While certain violations or allegations may seem routine given the size and nature of Stanford's enterprise, when a company has had multiple actions taken against it, there is definitely reason to use caution or at least ask questions before moving ahead with any business relationship.

Outside of the information reported to FINRA, in January 2008, two former employees of Stanford Group Company sued the firm for wrongful termination/employment discrimination and fraud in Harris County District Court, Texas. A review of the complaint filed in the case determined the plaintiffs were former financial advisors for high net worth clients at Stanford Group who became aware of illegal practices involving the sale of the company's certificates of deposit and other securities offerings. The plaintiffs requested that management comply with legal requirements, but when the firm refused, the plaintiffs were forced to resign in order to avoid participating in these illegal practices. As it turns out, these two former employees had testified before the SEC in 2007 before this case was filed. The complaint in this case provides an uncanny glimmer into the future as the

SEC's allegations against Stanford are very similar to the plaintiffs': that the company misrepresented the value of certificates of deposit.

For those of you not satisfied that claims of exaggerated returns are cause for concern, what about the term "Ponzi scheme?"

In March 2006, Stanford Financial Group was sued by a former employee in Miami-Dade County, Florida. The former employee alleged that the firm "was operating a 'Ponzi' or pyramid scheme, taking new money to its offshore bank, laundering the money and using the money to finance its growing brokerage business, which did not have any profits of its own." This was *not* the first time the term "Ponzi scheme" was used to describe Stanford Group.

In November 2005 a civil case was filed against Stanford Group Company and several affiliates in U.S. District Court, Southern District of Florida. The lawsuit was filed by two Venezuelan investors in Stanford who alleged that Stanford International Bank "knowingly aided and abetted...a classic Ponzi scheme," targeting current and former residents of Venezuela. Specifically, the plaintiffs alleged that Freddy Manzano, a co-defendant in the case, was a fugitive from Venezuela and was a perpetrator of a Ponzi scheme known as "La Vuelta," of which the plaintiffs were investors. The plaintiffs claim that Manzano used Stanford International as a bank for his funds and that Stanford International, through Stanford Financial, knew about the fraud yet still allowed Manzano to deposit his funds and issue sham promissory notes. The case was ultimately settled out of court.

Having established that Stanford Group has been accused of fraud, operating a Ponzi scheme, and misrepresenting information to investors, what else could *possibly* be out there in the public domain for investors to know about this company? You guessed it: money laundering.

In August 2002, Kadir Overseas Ltd. and Jorge Bastida Gallardo filed a federal-level civil case in Florida against Stanford Group Company and Stanford International Bank. The plaintiffs, who were, according to media articles, front men for the Mexican drug lord

Amado Carrillo Fuentes, alleged that Stanford Group failed to protect the launderers' money when the bank voluntarily gave $3 million
of the launderers' money to the U.S. Drug Enforcement Administration in cooperation with a narcotics investigation. Yes, there is
implicit comedy in the fact that money launderers used legitimate
legal channels to blame Stanford for not protecting their illegally
gained money and handing it over to authorities. Yet beyond that, the
statement is clear: Stanford Group was holding money for Mexican
money launderers. There were also several media articles published
that discussed Stanford's ties to these Mexican drug cartels.

The money laundering whispers spread beyond the ears of the
courtroom. In the late 1990s and into the 2000s, various news articles
tied U.S. government concerns regarding money laundering in Antigua
to Stanford's bank, given that Stanford International Bank was the
largest on the island and an established offshore banking center.
Antiguan leaders described Stanford as the "most influential" man on
the island. And while Sir Allen himself was not implicated in criminal
wrongdoing, he was at the center of a controversial 1998 overhaul of
Antigua's money laundering legislation. Antiguan Prime Minister Lester
Bird, with whom Stanford had a close relationship, personally asked
Stanford to lead the reform effort. The U.S. government complained
that new secrecy rules only deepened the country's reputation as a haven
for money laundering. Stanford's presence on the six-member regulatory authority, the United States said, was a conflict of interest. Subsequently, the Treasury Department issued a special advisory against
Antigua, warning banks to take extra precautions when handling transactions routed through there. Eventually, according to these media
reports, Antigua changed its banking laws substantially enough to be
dropped from a list of problematic offshore havens in 2001.

It is also interesting to consider that Stanford, like Bernie Madoff,
used a small accounting firm to oversee the bank's operations. The
accounting firm, C.A.S. Hewlett & Co., was based in Antigua and run
by Charlesworth (Shelley) Hewlett, who died in January 2009.

There was an enormous amount of information available in the public domain about Robert Allen Stanford and the activities of his companies. Had investors bothered to follow our suggested research methods (as laid out in the preceding pages of this book) and found out what transpired with Stanford's companies in the last few years, we doubt that any investor would have committed money to the Stanford-run financial institutions.

The Sting of Pang

So, what about Danny Pang? Danny Pang was a Taiwanese man who established offices in California and ran Private Equity Management Group (PEMG). In raising millions of dollars from investors, many of whom were from Taiwan, Pang abused his connections to the wealthy in Taiwan and relied on one talent: telling lies. In April 2009, the SEC filed a civil case against Danny Pang, stating he had defrauded investors of millions of dollars, and the SEC went so far as to freeze Pang's assets. Two weeks after the SEC's actions, the FBI arrested Pang, claiming he had deliberately structured his cash withdrawals in amounts under $10,000 so as to avoid notifying federal regulators, who had established the $10,000 mark as a means to identify money laundering activities. Five months after his house of cards crumbled, in September 2009 Danny Pang committed suicide.

In looking into Pang's background, we attempted to confirm the Master of Business Administration degree that Pang told investors he received from the University of California at Irvine. It seems Pang was the only one aware of this degree. The school said that while Danny Pang was enrolled for one class in the summer of 1986, he never attended any other classes, and he certainly never received an undergraduate or an MBA degree from this school.

We also sought to confirm other statements made in Pang's biography posted on PEMG's website. The bio stated Pang served on the

boards of "many" public companies. We scoured SEC filings and did
not find Pang as a member of the board of *any* publicly traded company. Further, we checked with the SEC and determined that Pang's
investment firm was not registered as an investment adviser, and Pang
was not individually registered with the SEC, FINRA, or any other
state or federal regulatory body. Again, this information is readily available on the SEC and FINRA websites and would have made any
investor realize that Pang was 0 for 2 in the game of truth and had deliberately not disclosed his activities to any appropriate regulatory agency.

Our next step was to see if Pang had been involved in any material lawsuits or court filings that would have given investors some clue
as to how Pang would use investor money. While we did not conduct
an inquiry in Taiwan, we did review court records in California and
found Pang as a defendant in several civil cases. Most notably, Pang
and one of his affiliates, InterPacific Capital, were sued for fraud in
April 2001 in Orange County Court. The case was not settled until
February 2006, five years after the case was filed. If the cause of
action is listed as fraud, racketeering, or if someone has been sued by
a financial institution, then investors definitely need to learn more
before moving forward.

Also, in September 2003 Pang was sued by Eagle Guo for breach
of contract, according to the case index information in Orange
County, California. At first glance, "breach of contract" did not appear
to be anything out of the ordinary. But we learned that "breach of
contract" was just one of the many causes of action in this case. Once
we reviewed the complaint filed in this case, we learned Eagle Guo,
the plaintiff, was an investor of Pang's who charged Pang with con-
structive fraud and damages for sale of unqualified securities, in addition to breach of contract. This investor claimed he gave Pang more
than $80,000 to be invested in a fund (later believed to be nonexist-
ent) and that Pang "absconded with" the money and used it for his
own personal gain. Had investors retrieved the court documents filed
in this case, they would have known that Pang had a history of

defrauding his earnest investors. Finally, in 1999 two financial institutions, Midland National Life and CitiCorp, filed lawsuits against Pang personally.

Erring on the side of trust and optimism, Pang theoretically could have lied about his education to get ahead, and then before he knew it, the lie had been going on for so many years that it became almost too late to come clean. And it is always possible the lawsuits filed against Pang were baseless, and maybe even that he was a target of prejudice against Taiwanese people. But what about the media articles published in 2002 that repeatedly state the FBI said Pang "might have" connections to the Taiwanese mob? Or that the president and CEO of Pang's former employer, Sky Capital Partners, alleged Pang stole $3 million and forged the CEO's signature? And then there are the disconcerting personal issues about Pang: that his former wife, Janie, was a stripper who once called the police to their house, alleging Pang had beat her and stole money from her parents. In 1997, Janie Pang was killed, at age 33, and to date, the killer is unknown. In 2002, the man who was charged with Janie Pang's murder admitted in court that he engaged in money laundering on behalf of Pang. The man was later found not guilty of killing Janie Pang.

Our tally of red flags identified for Pang so far include allegations of money laundering, theft, forgery, abuse, and deceit. This is all *before* the former employees of PEMG disclosed that Pang used investor money to buy a Gulfstream jet, and was even so bold as to tell some of his employees that he was engaged in a Ponzi scheme. Knowing all of this, would you have given Pang any of your money?

Pang Court Records

The court cases involving Pang *were* available online through the Orange County, California court system at www.occourts.org.

Remember Bayou?

Bayou Hedge Fund Group was a hedge fund founded by Sam Israel III, who pled guilty to defrauding investors of $450 million in 2005. As with Bernie Madoff and Robert Allen Stanford, investors quickly handed over money to Bayou with the hopes of unrealistic returns and overlooked the basic due diligence steps that would have given them plenty of information to suggest that investing with Mr. Israel was not a wise decision. When we researched Mr. Israel's background to find any clues that would predict the debacle that unfolded for investors in Bayou, we found was that Sam Israel significantly overstated his credentials regarding his tenure and his responsibilities at a prior employer. Of course, the lies and mismanagement do not end there.

Two former employees had sued Bayou, Mr. Israel, and Dan Marino (CFO) in March 2003 in Louisiana, two years before the fiasco. In reviewing the complaint filed in the case, we determined the former employees alleged that Bayou engaged in potential violations of both SEC and NASD (now known as FINRA) regulations. The complaint also mentions an inexplicable depletion of $7 million of company funds in December 2002. When the plaintiffs raised the issue of the missing monies to Mr. Israel, they were quickly fired from Bayou, according to the complaint.

Also, Dan Marino, the Bayou CFO, (not the famous Miami Dolphin quarterback of the same name) was the registered agent for the allegedly independent accounting firm used by Bayou. And in March 2005, Bayou hired a new Director of Investments. Well, this newly appointed director filed for Chapter 7 bankruptcy protection in May 1993 and then *again* filed for Chapter 13 bankruptcy protection in California in April 2002. Would you hire him to direct your investments if he clearly cannot direct his own?

Last, we found Dan Marino had sued a fund in the Isle of Man in March 2003, alleging the principals of the fund had engaged in fraud and misrepresentation. A review of the complaint in the case determined Mr. Marino had given $2 million to this fund. Had investors known about this case, they would have immediately questioned the origin of the $2 million investment and would have wanted to know more about Dan Marino and Bayou's connections to a fund that allegedly engaged in fraud.

The public record information available on Stanford Group Company, Danny Pang, and Bayou is much more abundant and blatantly damaging than for Bernie Madoff. However, the commonalities between Robert Allen Stanford, Danny Pang, and Bernie Madoff are that they each used their reputations, whether fabricated or true, to keep investors in the dark. We call this "flock funding." Investors relied on reputation and not research when they invested: They followed the flock. Bernie's reputation was supported and echoed by a vast network of friends and family; Stanford's reputation was established through tight friendships with influential government heads both offshore and on; and Pang's reputation was built from his connections to his homeland in Taiwan. Another shared and critical trait: The information and warning signs were out there to be found, had anyone been interested in looking.

And the Moral of the Story Is...

In 2008 and 2009, as the economy faltered and once-revered financial institutions crumbled, instances of corporate fraud were being announced on a weekly basis. In this chapter, we discussed some of the largest frauds that were revealed during this time period: Madoff, Stanford, and Pang. But it is important to know that defrauding investors is not and probably will not be limited to this time frame. An article in *Time* magazine, dated June 10, 1985, entitled "Crime in the Suites," stated

The way things are going, *Fortune* may soon have to publish a 500 Most Wanted list. During the past few months the news has been filled with tales of business schemes and scandals, of corporate intrigue and downright crime. The offenses make up a catalog of chicanery: cheating on government defense contracts, check-writing fraud, bogus securities dealing, tax dodges, insider trading and money laundering... But rarely have so many big-name businessmen and corporations been accused of so much wrongdoing in so short a time. Several business trends, including financial deregulation, the growth of huge conglomerates and the rise of electronic funds transfers, seem to be multiplying the opportunities and temptations for businessmen to stray outside the law.

All you have to do is change a few of the types of crime named in this paragraph, and the statements apply today. The 1985 article discussed the corporate crime that was prevalent in the 1980s. Most of these crimes, such as insider trading and money laundering, remain issues of concern. And while state and federal regulators scramble to implement revamped rules to accommodate the most recent waves of corporate fraud, there are always loopholes. Within weeks of the implementation of the 2008 Troubled Asset Relief Program (TARP), a special inspector general was appointed to monitor potential fraud in the program. By April 2009, there were 20 investigations being pursued involving alleged TARP fraud, and in March 2010, the CEO of Park Avenue Bank, located in New York City, was arrested for engaging in such fraud. This was the first time criminal charges were brought against an executive for violations of TARP rules. The CEO allegedly lied about his bank's financial status in order to illegally get a piece of the TARP bailout money.

Creative corporate criminals will continue to find ways to permeate the system in their desperate journeys for wealth, power, or whatever drives them. To avoid becoming a victim, the answer does not lie in fear or apathy; paranoia is as helpful as ignorance. Rather, your survival rests in your awareness. Information is your advocate.

The cases discussed in this book have one common theme: disclosure. When information was withheld, the success of a deal or investment was compromised. From Bernie Madoff's billion-dollar Ponzi scheme to a slight exaggeration on a resume, when information is not properly disclosed, the balance of power is shifted to those in the know and those being duped. The end result is always that reputations and bank accounts are greatly sacrificed. Transparency is vital in every transaction, whether in the United States or overseas.

The purpose of telling these stories from our arsenal of investigations is certainly not to instill fear, but rather to impart caution. The objective of the background check is to confirm someone's good name and to bring to your attention any discrepancies, controversies, reputational issues, or potential problems that may impact the prosperity of your deal. We are relieved when we conduct a background check and find the person has a clean slate and accurately represented himself. Background checks should always be used and assessed in conjunction with your legal and financial due diligence. The intelligence we gather is designed to protect you and give you the confidence and knowledge to move forward with your transaction, whatever that may be. Background checks give you intelligence, which in turn gives you the power to act judiciously.

Resource Guide

Resources discussed throughout the book:

Source Name	Type of Info	How to Access
Securities and Exchange Commission (SEC)	Investment Adviser Search	www.adviserinfo.sec.gov
Financial Industry Regulatory Authority (FINRA)	Registered brokers and securities firms; violations; censures, etc.	www.finra.org
National Futures Association (NFA)	Registered individuals and firms in futures business; disciplinary actions filed by NFA and Commodity Futures Trading Commission (CFTC)	www.nfa.futures.org
Financial Services Authority (FSA)	Registered individuals and firms in the securities industry in the United Kingdom; disciplinary actions, etc.	www.fsa.gov.uk

Source Name	Type of Info	How to Access
Securities and Futures Commission (SFC)	Registered individuals and firms in securities and futures in Hong Kong; disciplinary actions ("Alert List")	www.sfc.hk
Chicago Board Options Exchange (CBOE)	Disciplinary actions taken by this agency	http://www.cboe.org/legal/discipAction.aspx
PACER	Federal-level civil, criminal, and bankruptcy filings and appeals cases	http://pacer.psc.uscourts.gov/
National Student Clearinghouse	Verify degrees and attendance at colleges and universities	www.studentclearinghouse.org/
Delaware Secretary of State	Corporate records for entities formed in Delaware	http://corp.delaware.gov
New Jersey Secretary of State	Corporate records for entities formed in New Jersey	https://accessnet.state.nj.us/home.asp
Federal Bureau of Prisons	Inmate locator system to access records on individuals who have been incarcerated	www.bop.gov/iloc2/LocateInmate.jsp
California Sex Offender Registry	To determine if a person is a known sex offender in California	www.meganslaw.ca.gov/
New York Sex Offender Registry	To determine if a person is a known sex offender in New York	http://criminaljustice.state.ny.us/nsor/

Source Name	Type of Info	How to Access
BRB Publications	Information on state-level courts (counties, websites, etc.)	www.brbpub.com
National Archives and Records Administration	Confirm military service	www.archives.gov
Federal Election Commission	Identify political donations made by individuals and companies	www.fec.gov
Campaign Contributions	Other ways to search for political donations	opensecrets.org newsmeat.com followthemoney.org campaignmoney.com
Federal Aviation Administration (FAA)	Identify pilot's licenses and private planes owned by an individual or company	www.faa.gov
Better Business Bureau (BBB)	Identify consumer complaints filed against companies	www.bbb.org
Occupational Safety & Health Administration (OSHA)	Identify complaints, violations, and inspections filed against a company	www.osha.gov
General Services Administration (GSA)	Identify companies excluded from receiving government contracts	https://www.epls.gov/
Office of Foreign Assets Control (OFAC)	Identify sanctions filed against individuals or companies who are in violation of U.S. policies and engage in business overseas	www.ustreas.gov/offices/ enforcement/ofac/

Source Name	Type of Info	How to Access
U.S. Patent and Trademark Office	Identify patents and trademarks assigned to and developed by individuals and companies	www.uspto.gov/
Federal Trade Commission (FTC)	Identify actions taken against companies in violation of U.S. trade policies	www.ftc.gov
Environmental Protection Agency (EPA)	Identify actions taken by the EPA against companies engaged in industries that impact the environment	www.epa.gov
U.S. Department of Education	Names of accrediting agencies to contact to confirm a school is not a diploma mill	www.ed.gov
Federal Communications Commission (FCC)	Identify information, licenses, complaints, etc. for companies in media (radio, broadcast, telephone, Internet, and so on)	www.fcc.gov
Way Back Machine	View archived websites to identify discrepancies in corporate biographies, etc.	www.archive.org
WHOIS	Domain name registrations	www.networksolutions.com/whois/index.jsp
U.S. Tax Court	Identify cases filed by or against the Internal Revenue Service	www.ustaxcourt.gov

Source Name	Type of Info	How to Access
Insider Trading Database	Tracks holdings in publicly traded companies	http://research.thomsonib.com/
Guidestar	Information on nonprofit entities	http://www2.guidestar.org/
Bloomberg	We have a Bloomberg terminal, but Bloomberg has a news division on the website that deals primarily with financial news	www.bloomberg.com
Factiva	Dow Jones publications	http://factiva.com/
Westlaw	Thomson/Reuters publications, court records, court documents, and other information	www.westlaw.com
Lexis/Nexis	Property records; corporate records; media sources; miscellaneous information	www.lexisnexis.com

To access some of these resources, you must purchase an account.

This list does not include all of the sources that can be used in an investigation.

INDEX

G–H

FINANCIAL TIMES

In an increasingly competitive world, it is quality
of thinking that gives an edge—an idea that opens new
doors, a technique that solves a problem, or an insight
that simply helps make sense of it all.

We work with leading authors in the various arenas
of business and finance to bring cutting-edge thinking
and best-learning practices to a global market.

It is our goal to create world-class print publications
and electronic products that give readers
knowledge and understanding that can then be
applied, whether studying or at work.

To find out more about our business
products, you can visit us at www.ftpress.com.